CREATION TO REVELATION

CREATION TO REVELATION

A Brief Account of the Biblical Story

James O. Chatham

William B. Eerdmans Publishing Company

Grand Rapids, Michigan / Cambridge, U.K.

To Nancy,

    the treasure of my life!

© 2006 James O. Chatham
All rights reserved

Published 2006 by
Wm. B. Eerdmans Publishing Co.
2140 Oak Industrial Drive N.E., Grand Rapids, Michigan 49505 /
P.O. Box 163, Cambridge CB3 9PU U.K.

Printed in the United States of America

11 10 09 08 07 06   7 6 5 4 3 2 1

Library of Congress Cataloging-in-Publication Data

Chatham, James O., 1937-
    Creation to Revelation: a brief account of the biblical story / James O. Chatham.
        p.   cm.
    Includes index.
    ISBN-10: 0-8028-6322-1 / ISBN-13: 978-0-8028-6322-5 (pbk.: alk. paper)
    1. Bible — Criticism, interpretation, etc.   2. Bible — History of Biblical events.
    I. Title.

    BS511.3.C43 2006
    220.9'5 — dc22

                                                            2006021875

www.eerdmans.com

Contents

CONTENTS

1

Introduction

This book tells in broad strokes the entire biblical story, "from creation to Revelation," so that lay readers can get a view of the whole.

Many Christians have favorite passages from the Bible: "The Lord is my shepherd," from Psalm 23; "For God so loved the world," from John 3; "Love is not jealous or boastful," from 1 Corinthians 13. Some even know that Jeremiah lamented deeply the waywardness of God's people, or that Luke rejoiced that God was enlarging the church beyond Israel. But few have a clear picture of the full biblical story. Few are able to read a particular text from within the context of the whole. One purpose of this book is to begin to address that challenge in a short, readable way.

In our time, the danger of reading single biblical texts in isolation has become apparent. We have all encountered individuals — perhaps politicians, televangelists, or even people we know — who piece together a small handful of texts that appear to support their particular ideology, whatever it is. Such persons then declare those few texts to be authoritative, God's definitive word, a firm "biblical principle." And they end up using those few texts to vilify opponents, demonize enemies, attack anyone they consider to be opposed to God. All this from a book that calls us to love and forgiveness and reconciliation and peace!

Many of our theological ancestors insisted on measuring what any individual biblical text says against what they heard all biblical texts saying. They called it consulting "the whole counsel of God." A starchy verse from Revelation 19 that speaks of a cosmic whore who is to be devoured with fire, in other words, should probably not be taken as urging us to start identifying cosmic whores and burning them, but rather should be transcended by the fact that, across the Bible, God's relation to whores (whether individuals who were literally engaged in the business of prostitution, like Rahab, or entire societies that had strayed from fidelity to God, like Israel in the Book of Hosea) had mostly to do with claiming them for some significant role in the divine plan.

To know the whole Bible story, in other words, is critical to a faithful interpretation of individual texts.

The Bible was written over a period of approximately twelve hundred years. Its authors included rural farmers, sophisticated urbanites, poets, historians, storytellers, prophets, people clutched in the tight grip of foreign domination, exiles, slaves set free, individuals with great faith, and individuals with great doubt. From this disparate array of authors comes a huge range of expressions — expressions that often reinforce but sometimes contradict one another. It is not unusual for Scripture to argue with Scripture, for text to conflict with text.

But despite this diversity, the Bible bears a persistent unity, a oneness throughout. From cover to cover, it relates a single tale, the tale of one God, its main subject, and of one humanity, its second subject. The God who is "from everlasting to everlasting" moves throughout, along with a humanity that changes only cosmetically. Through vastly different times and circumstances, God's oneness and our oneness create the one Bible story.

And we cannot help but respond in some way to this story. Objectivity is not an option. A voice speaks, calling, beckoning, laying claim, challenging the way our world is configured, questioning how we think and live. We cannot read the Bible and walk away; it asks for engagement. Another one of my purposes in this book is to articulate the claim I hear the whole Bible story making on us.

* * *

Before we begin, a word about the structure of this book and how you may want to read it. I will begin by sketching biblical geography, showing major contours of the Holy Land as well as major contours of the human minds it produced. From there we will move through the entire biblical story, from creation to Revelation, relating the most significant events and highlighting meaning. In the final two chapters I will set forth my understanding of the meaning of this story that stretches from the Bible's beginning to its end.

I have placed liberally throughout the book a variety of sidebars. Some sidebars offer reflections I think are pertinent to the story. Others report events going on in other parts of the world while the biblical story was taking place.

At the end of the book, I have placed two appendixes. Appendix A, "Chronology of the Bible's Story," attaches possible or likely dates to events covered in the book. The reader should know that while some dates are quite dependable (for example, we know for a fact that Jerusalem was destroyed by the Babylonians in 587 B.C.E.), other dates derive from speculation (such as that Jesus was born in 4 B.C.E. and died in 29 C.E.) since the sources are sparse and usually not concerned with precise dating.

In Appendix B, I have placed daily Bible readings, fourteen of them for each study unit. This assumes (somewhat arbitrarily) that you will spend a year studying through the book, devoting two weeks to each study unit. The Bible readings are texts most closely related to the study unit. They will support your work.

You can read this book by yourself or in a group. If you can read with a group, I recommend it. I have divided the text into twenty-six study segments, of which this introduction is the first. After each study segment, a "For Deliberation" section is meant to guide your thinking and discussion. Don't feel compelled to discuss all the questions; pick the ones most pertinent to you.

My main purpose in writing this book is to help the Bible come alive in your life as it has in mine. The Bible is not a dead book, mired in the irrelevant thought forms of primitive history. It is your story and my story, yesterday, today, tomorrow; and it is the story of God, who walks silently and invisibly, but pervasively, with us. If I can make that point, even as I teach you the main events, I will have succeeded.

Please know that this book is no substitute for reading the Bible itself. The Bible speaks its word and lays its claim far better than I can. This book is but an introduction; please use it that way.

A brief word on what this book is not. It is not a survey of recent interpretations of biblical literature. Scholars are constantly rereading biblical texts and suggesting new variations on understanding them. (One text receiving attention right now, for instance, is the story of the Tower of Babel, to make it less a tale of the depths of human sinfulness and more of God's blessing of human diversity.) A survey of current text interpretations is very valuable and creates worthwhile reading. But it is not what I am doing. I am writing an introductory book for laypeople. I am presenting how I, a biblical teacher for nearly forty years, currently understand this book, and what I, a preacher, believe it says and means. You are reading here the sense I make of it all. I find that to be the most valuable thing I can impart to my fellow believers.

FOR DELIBERATION

1. The Bible develops for us a picture of God, a rendering of what we can know about the Holy One. The Bible also develops a picture of us, a portrait of the people we are and of how we act. As you begin this study, make a brief list of the most significant things you already understand the Bible to say about God — for example, "God loves us." "God is like a shepherd who walks with us through the valley of the shadow of death." "God can get very angry over some of the things we do." These are just a few possibilities. Continue making this list as you work through this book.

2. Similarly, list several things the Bible says about us. "We eat forbidden fruit." "We can be heroically faithful, even at the risk of our lives." "We can be disgustingly unfaithful and self-centered." These are just some ideas. Continue making this list, too, as you work through this book.

3. Name two or three of your favorite passages from the Bible. How well do these texts reflect your overall picture of God? Where are they inadequate?

4. One of the most important insights of biblical scholarship over the past century has been to realize how important it is to know what type of literature we are reading. We would not read a newspaper editorial the same way we read a comic strip, or a news story, or an obituary. Knowing the literary type is very important for our comprehension (scholars call it "form criticism"). What sort of literature would you expect from each of the following: a poet, a historian, a storyteller, a prophet, people clutched in the tight grip of foreign domination, slaves set free? What would you look for from each of these authors? What would you not look for?

5. Name one or two biblical texts that you believe have been or could be badly misused to violate the spirit of the Bible. (For example, because Matthew 5:30 says, "If your right hand causes you to sin, cut it off," there have been a few Christians who have done exactly that!)

6. Read Deuteronomy 21:18-21. Now read Luke 15:11-24. How do these two texts "argue with" each other? What is one implying about the relation between parents and children? What is the other implying? Is there something worthwhile to be heard from each?

7. Now read the story of the temptation of Jesus in Luke 4:1-15. The devil quotes scripture to Jesus; Jesus quotes other scripture to the devil. How do these scriptures "argue with" one another?

2

Contours of the Land

The land of Israel, where the Bible's story takes place, is located on the eastern shore of the Mediterranean Sea, south of present-day Lebanon and Syria and northeast of Egypt. The map on page 8 shows the territory. The map on the facing page shows the same territory in modern times.

For a territory that has been so momentous and consequential in the history of the world, the land of Israel is tiny, scarcely larger than two-thirds the size of the state of Vermont. In the Bible, the term "from Dan to Beersheba" is used to mean "all Israel," Dan being a town at the northern tip and Beersheba in the far south. The two locations are a mere 145 miles apart. The east-west distance from the Mediterranean Sea to the Jordan River ranges between 35 and 60 miles. A great advantage for travelers visiting Israel today is that each major site is often no more than fifteen minutes' drive from the one previous. You don't have to spend most of your day getting from place to place.

Formidable mountain ranges run north and south through the center of the country, bordered by the coastal plain of the Mediterranean on the west and the similarly flat Jordan River Valley on the east. The Valley of Jezreel, an expanse of fertile land, occupies the north-central region. Since both horses and wheeled fighting vehicles function better on flat land than on steep hillsides, the Valley of Jezreel has, throughout history, been a good location for farmers to grow their food and for armies to fight their battles.

Israel is a place of height extremes. The land surrounding the Dead Sea is 1,600 feet below sea level, the lowest area of dry ground on earth. Jerusalem, a scant fifteen miles to the west, is over 2,000 feet above sea level, atop the north-south mountain range. The adjoining route, the road from Jerusalem to Jericho (where Jesus set his famous story about the Good Samaritan), is a steep and winding twist.

In all its thousands of years of human habitation, one factor has been the key to success or failure in the region of Israel: fresh water. Those who have it can survive and thrive. Those who have it in great abundance can become wealthy and powerful. Those who have little of it are forever destined to subsistence at best.

Rainfall amounts in Israel vary radically from north to south, even though the distance is less than that from Dallas to Austin. In the north, in the Valley of Jezreel and above, as much as forty inches of rain can fall in a year, almost all of it in winter. Good growing seasons are regular and vegetation prospers. In the south, the Negev Desert can receive as little as one inch of rain per year. The Negev is resplendent in its rich, earth-tone dryness, with vivid yellows and rusts and coppers and reds and tans. One gazes nearly in vain to see what the Bedouin shepherds that roam the region are finding to eat. Jerusalem, situated about midway between Jezreel and the Negev, averages twenty-two inches of rainfall per year.

The Mediterranean Sea borders Israel on the west, but its salty waters are useless for sustaining human life. (Those who know how can fish it, but the ancient Israelites were not seafarers, as we will see.) The Sea of Galilee, the Jordan River, and the Dead Sea are all to the east. Galilee and Jordan offer the best supplies of fresh water in the region, although at some points the Jordan is little wider than a large creek. The Dead Sea, a very unusual body of water, is heavy with salt and minerals. No fish can live in it, and its water is unsuitable for drinking.

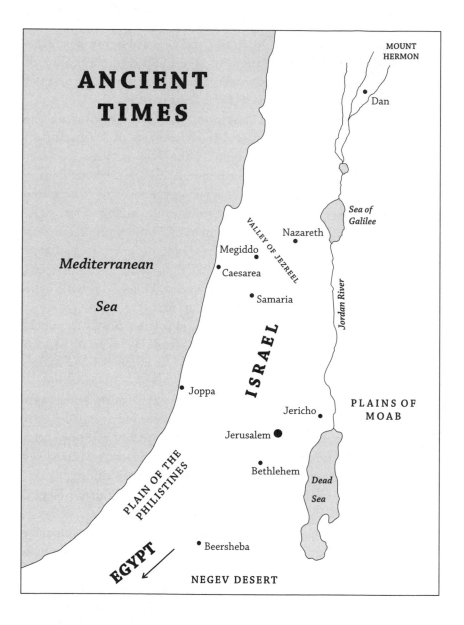

ANCIENT
TIMES

MOUNT
HERMON

Dan

Sea of
Galilee

VALLEY OF JEZREEL

Nazareth

Megiddo

Mediterranean

Caesarea

Sea

Samaria

Jordan River

ISRAEL

PLAINS OF
MOAB

Joppa

Jericho

Jerusalem

Bethlehem

PLAIN OF THE
PHILISTINES

Dead
Sea

EGYPT

Beersheba

NEGEV DESERT

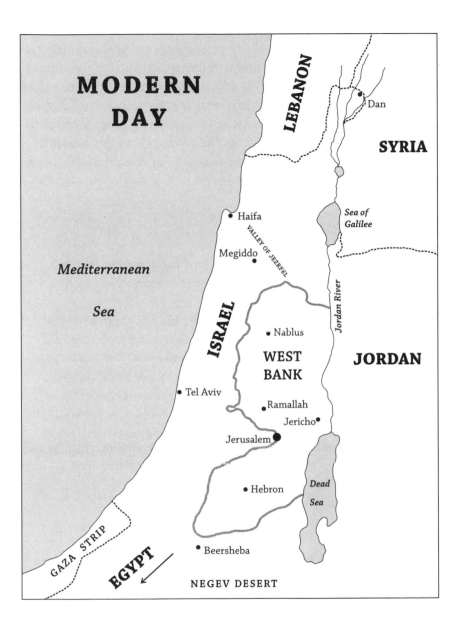

The entire region of Israel sits atop a series of subterranean basins that collect rainwater and send it generously back to the surface. Thus, a spring high in the hills will pour forth cooling water that makes its way toward the sea or river valley below by way of a creek, or "wadi," bestowing refreshment on every living thing in its path. The prophet Elijah took refuge from the anger of King Ahab by hiding by one of these wadis, and thus he was able to remain in the desert without dying of thirst (see 1 Kings 17).

RAIN

Louisville, Kentucky, where I live, averages nearly forty-six inches of rain per year and sometimes receives as much as sixty. What about your location?

Given the near-drought conditions many people on earth experience, I try not to disparage a single drop of rain, no matter how personally inconvenient it may be.

Friends of ours recently adopted two five-year-old girls from an orphanage in Ethiopia. The greatest fascination these two little girls found in their new home was — would you believe it? — tap water, fresh drinking water any time they wanted it. They would stand at the sink and run it through their fingers just to enjoy the feel!

Likewise, King David undoubtedly picked Jerusalem to be his capital city for two reasons. First, because it sits atop a precipice that is essentially unapproachable from three sides, making it easy to defend in wartime. Second, because the Spring of Gihon provided a steady supply of fresh water near the hilltop. Gihon nourished the Holy City for generations, until the population finally grew so large that water had to be imported.

Visitors to Israel today are often surprised, while traveling through some expanse of relatively dry and sparse countryside, to suddenly encounter a postage stamp of brilliant green, several hundred to a few thousand acres of lush grasses and trees and vines and cultivated crops. The explanation? The Israelis will have found a water basin beneath the ground and pumped the precious liquid to the surface for irrigation, literally causing the desert to bloom.

Despite its wadis and springs and the ingenuity of the people, the land of Israel has always desperately lacked fresh water. With the possible exception of the shoreline of the Sea of Galilee, no part of Israel has ever had enough water to support a large population. True wealth and international power, in ancient times, were therefore out of the question.

By contrast, two other ancient Near Eastern societies possessed huge supplies of fresh water, and both became political and cultural superpowers. Egypt, to the southwest of Israel, was supplied by the Nile River, a 3,500-mile waterway that begins in the highlands of east-central Africa and flows northward to the Mediterranean. Its one-million-square-mile watershed receives heavy rain. The dependably steady flow, along with the Nile's periodic flooding, made Egypt the bread basket of the ancient Near East, where Israelites and many others repeatedly sought food when their own countries experienced drought and famine.

The Tigris and Euphrates Rivers, in present-day Iraq, also provide plentiful fresh water. The region around those rivers produced two international powers during the biblical era: Assyria, whose capital was Nineveh on the upper Tigris; and Babylon, based around the Tigris-Euphrates junction near the Persian Gulf.

Assyria, Babylon, and Egypt were the ancient superpowers. They mustered powerful armies from their populations and possessed the wealth to support conquest. Fortunately and unfortunately, Israel lay directly between them.

It was fortunate because, in times of international peace, Israel sat at the intersection of well-traveled trade routes. Merchants came not only from Egypt and Assyria but also from Arabia in the southeast and Mesopotamia in the northwest, bringing such products as fine pottery, perfumes, spices, horses, exotic foods, oils, musical in-

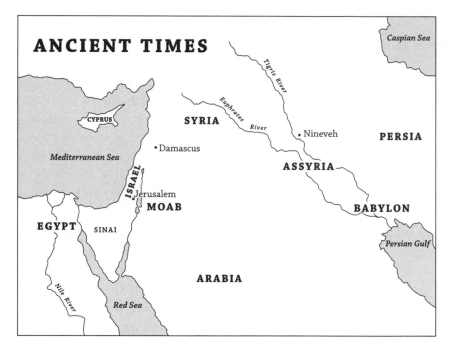

struments, and even monkeys (which were kept by wealthy people as entertainment). Israel was able to levy tariffs for the use of the routes. Two of the most prosperous eras in Israel's life, under King Solomon in the tenth century B.C.E. and under King Jeroboam II in the eighth, were both fueled primarily by trade wealth.

But Israel's location was unfortunate because, in times of conflict, the nation became easy prey for the advancing powers. Time and again, foreign armies fought on Israelite territory, destroying towns, looting temples, ravaging fields, killing populations. It was like life on a volcano: the next upheaval was impossible to predict, but certain to come.

This land of beauty and uncertainty, of miraculous springs and harsh deserts, is the setting for the Bible's story. In the next chapter we will look at the kind of people it produced.

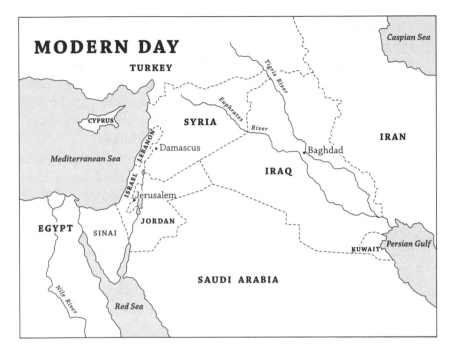

For Deliberation

1. Can you name similarly small land areas elsewhere on earth that have made huge contributions to human history, human faith, and human self-understanding? The novelist Edward Rutherford wrote a book entitled *Sarum,* which, by combining fiction and history, sought to highlight the pivotal role of Salisbury Plain in southern England in the development of Western civilization. Can you think of other small locations that have been important through centuries of time?

2. Try to draw from memory the map of the Holy Land contained in this chapter. If you are studying in a group, you might have one person draw the Sea of Galilee, the next person the Jordan River, the next the Dead Sea, and so forth. Can you fix in mind the main contours of the land?

3. Compare ancient and modern maps of the Holy Land. Notice how the land is divided between Israelis and Palestinians, who have had a very tense relationship since 1948, when many Palestinians were driven away from their homes and made refugees by Israel's claiming of the land. From examining the maps, can you think of any geographical factors that would add to the volatility of the relationship between the Israelis and the Palestinians?

4. Has there ever been a time when you were severely thirsty and could find no water? How did your body and mind react? How would your life be different if you lacked an adequate supply of water?

5. Read Isaiah 19:23-25. In Isaiah's time, the two greatest military and economic powers were Egypt and Assyria, and they were constantly at each other's throats. Isaiah might well have prophesied that God would destroy them both, in retribution for their repeated violence against smaller nations. But instead, Isaiah prophesied that God would reconcile them, building between them a highway of peace, causing them to worship together. Isaiah's prophecy clearly came from his faith in God, not from any realistic evaluation of the bloody and violent era in which he lived. What must Isaiah have believed about God to cause him to draw this unlikely conclusion?

3

Contours of the Mind

The unique geographical features of the land of Israel produced a people with a similarly unique mindset. The Israelites were hill people, mountaineers, a population that knew very well how to negotiate heights and depths and slopes and turns, how to find level areas and cultivate them, how to communicate from hillside to hillside, how to live in small, close-knit villages and towns.

But these same people nearly froze with anxiety when they encountered large bodies of water. They were not sea people. Some of them might go fishing on the Sea of Galilee, a few even earning a living from it, but even these few kept a very wary eye on the hilltops on the western shore to see what might be blowing across. Storms at sea terrified them. They envisioned monsters and dragons and other giant creatures beneath the water, causing it to churn and rage. God alone, they believed, had the power to arouse or calm the sea and its creatures. This deep apprehension about sea sailing factors into many parts of the Bible's story.

Food anxiety was another major component of the Israelite mindset. Most people knew from personal experience how quickly and in how many ways a food supply could disappear: by drought, locusts, wild animals, blight, theft, consumption by a foreign army, or simply by the unpredictabilities of a poor growing season. A food stock could vanish instantly, and a whole population could be left desperate. Severe hunger was a condition almost everyone had experienced. Those few who had not certainly heard vivid tales about it from their parents or grandparents.

Food was God's precious gift. Meals were cause for thanksgiving. Feasts were reason for celebration. Nothing that could be eaten was wasted. *Enough* was a cherished experience that reached deeply into the soul. Those who had it knew they had been graciously blessed.

WONDER

If a Hebrew from the tenth century B.C.E. were magically to materialize in today's world, I am certain that his or her greatest source of wonder would not be the Sears Tower, nor antibiotics, nor television, nor automobiles, nor space rockets, nor cyberspace. It would be the modern grocery store: shelves upon shelves of food where, at any hour, in any season, one can find more than enough for everyone. You and I presume food. We easily come to think that, in the words of one flippant commentator, "Food is!" No ancient Hebrew would have taken food for granted.

The great contributions ancient Israelites made to history were not in the realm of architecture. Not far from Israel, the Egyptians had built pyramids and mausoleums and temples that would endure for millennia, awing the world with their engineering prowess. And a few hundred miles in another direction, the Greeks and Romans were hard at work constructing meeting halls and amphitheaters and coliseums and streets and cities that would endure as their legacy. Israelites built plenty of stone structures, some of them massive, but today's visitors to the Holy Land do not view samples of ancient engineering genius. The structures still standing came mostly from the Roman period or much later.

Instead, literature, poetry, and religious faith are the legacy of the ancient Israelites. Delicately told stories that speak perceptively of the human plight, poetic verse that traces human emotion through joy and perplexity, prayers that cry out toward heaven, epic tales that weave meaning and promise across generations — these were the Hebrew gift. Here are just a few of the most famous examples:

> Even though I walk through the valley of the shadow of death,
>   I fear no evil,
> for thou art with me.
>
> (Psalm 23:4, RSV)

> Love is patient; love is kind; love is not envious or boastful or arrogant or rude. It does not insist on its own way; it is not irritable or resentful; it does not rejoice in wrongdoing, but rejoices in the truth (1 Corinthians 13:4-6).

> Then the eyes of the blind shall be opened,
>   and the ears of the deaf unstopped;
> then shall the lame leap like a hart,
>   and the tongue of the dumb shall sing for joy!
>
> (Isaiah 35:5-6, RSV)

> Those who wait for the Lord shall renew their strength,
>   they shall mount up with wings like eagles,
> they shall run and not be weary,
>   they shall walk and not faint.
>
> (Isaiah 40:31)

> Lord, I believe; help thou my unbelief. (Mark 9:24)

These are among the enduring treasures ancient Israel left to the future. All of them are thousands of years old, yet they speak to us where we are today.

Even more than literature, the Israelites left to the world their faith — specifically, monotheistic faith. Faith that there is only one God at the source of everything, that the universe does not consist of a variety of spiritual powers competing for dominion. The peoples that surrounded ancient Israel worshipped many different gods, believing that each aspect of the natural world — the sun, the rain, the fertility of the soil — was controlled by a different deity. There were times when Israel found these polytheistic religions very appealing, no more so than when they encountered the fertility gods of the Canaanites who invited cultic prostitution as worship. Several prophets, Elijah at the head of the line, proclaimed mightily against these practices. For at the core of Israelite faith stood the conviction that a single God was the source of everything, the creator and sustainer of the entire universe, that the God of beauty and prosperity and blessing and hope was also in some mysterious way the God of violence and pain and suffering and death. It is, they told us, in facing this great mystery — of how both victory and defeat can be the domain of a single deity — that you and I will finally discern the truth about both God and ourselves.

Along with their monotheism came their faith in *one humanity,* faith that there is only one *us.* Faith that all people are born of the same parents, dwell in the same family, and share the same essential qualities. Faith that human life is not to be understood in terms of good people versus evil people, but rather that all human beings are in essence alike and will one day be united under God. Faith that reconciliation rather than triumphalism is God's direction. This is not to say that ancient Israel always lived by this faith. They, like virtually every nation throughout history, waged war, and there was often rampant injustice in their society. Those things, as well, are part of the Bible's story. But belief in the unity of humanity stood always at the core of their faith, surfacing strongly at different times and through different voices. These beliefs, in *one God* and in *one us,* were radically different from the beliefs of surrounding cultures. They stand at the heart of the Hebrew contribution to our world.

FOR DELIBERATION

1. Think about the geographical features of the region where you live. What is it like? What aspects of the local mindset have been shaped by that geography? How might you think differently if you lived somewhere else, somewhere with a very different climate or landscape?

2. When you are riding in a boat, does choppy water not bother you? Or are you like the ancient Hebrews, melting in fear with every swell? Can your mind imagine giant dragons and beasts beneath the water, hurling you about with their passions? What would you think if someone in your boat spoke to the waves and said, "Peace; be still," and suddenly there was "a great calm"? (See Mark 4:35-41.)

3. Talk about monotheistic faith. How would our faith, our view of the world, be different if we believed that different gods controlled different aspects of life? How would we think about other people differently? How would we think about tragedy and loss? What are the hard challenges of believing in one God as the creator and ruler of all events and all nations?

4. If people in the year 3000 look back at our culture, for what do you think we will be most prominently remembered? Our science? Our engineering? Our democracy? Our wealth? Our generosity? Our fear? For what would you most like our society to be remembered?

4

The Beginning: Good!

The story told by the Bible is, first and foremost, the story of God: God's words, God's acts, God's motives, God's emotions, God's manner, God's purpose. Human beings also play a significant role, but God — often subtly and sometimes openly — is the major actor.

Despite all the Bible tells us about God, God remains primarily a mystery. Far more shrouded in smoke than revealed. Far more transcendent than immanent. Beyond our vision and certainly beyond our comprehension. We can, as the prophet Isaiah suggests (Isa. 6:1), occasionally glimpse the hem of God's garment, but there is infinitely more that we do not learn about God than that we do. In Isaiah's words again, "As the heavens are higher than the earth, so are my ways higher than your ways and my thoughts than your thoughts, [says the Lord]" (Isa. 55:9). Paul says, "Now we see in a mirror dimly"; it will only be in a time to come that "we will see [God] face to face" (1 Cor. 13:12).

People of faith sometimes make the grievous error of claiming to understand God more fully than any human being can, of claiming that *we know* God's mind so authoritatively that we can now act as God's unquestionable representatives here on earth, telling the world with great certainty what is right and what is wrong, who is good and who is evil, who will go to heaven and who will be left behind. This is idolatry! We are mortal, and none of us is that connected with the Almighty.

But, still, we do see. The Bible is revelation. And, in fact, the church has believed through the ages that we see "enough." The revelation is sufficient for us to know what sort of God God is and what sort of people God calls us to be. We cannot see everything, but we can discern sufficiently. That ability to discern is what the Bible story provides.

The Bible is sometimes described as a record of humanity's search for God. This may be true in a sense, but it is far more true to say that the Bible tells of God's search for us. God pursues us, tracks us, claims us, calls us. I wonder sometimes why God wants us so badly. With our stubborn, stiff-necked, self-absorbed nature, why does God persist? The reason is buried deep in God's being, having to do with the fundamental quality that is God's essence: love. God will not desert us to our own devices because God loves us. As much as a shepherd who searches every crevice and ravine seeking his lost sheep or a woman who turns her house upside down to recover a lost coin, God loves us. "The good news of the gospel," the theologian Reinhold Niebuhr used to say, "is that we have found at the center of the universe a heart of love!"

The discovery of God's love created the Bible. The Bible is the story of God's seeking, searching, forgiving, claiming, redeeming love, and of the way God has woven that love through a community's life.

Here, then, is an overview of that story, the story from which both our faith and the church were born.

Genesis 1–11 tells of the beginning, the story of creation, and of how that creation went from being God's good and perfect handiwork to being the flawed, embattled place it is now.

God began (Gen. 1:1-5) with a watery chaos, a dark, formless, uncontrolled deep. The image of watery darkness would have been frightening indeed to the ancient Hebrews who were the first hearers of this story. Yet the creative Spirit of God moved over that deep.

Then God spoke. That was the beginning of creation: a word from the mouth of God. The word of God would henceforth be the most powerful, the most creative, the most persistent subject in the biblical story.

GOD'S WORD

"As the rain and snow come down from heaven and do not return there until they have watered the earth, . . . so shall be my word that goes forth from my mouth; it shall not return to me empty, but it shall accomplish that which I purpose" (Isa. 55:10-11). The ancient Hebrews believed that the word of God embodied an intention, a power, a purpose that no earthly restraint could stop. The word of God *would accomplish* whatever it spoke.

God said, "Let there be light," and there was light. God said, "Let there be a firmament in the midst of the waters," and there was a firmament. God said, "Let there be dry land," and there was dry land. With words, God created everything in six days, resting on the seventh (Gen. 1:1-2:4a).

After each day of creation, God evaluated the product and declared it "good." "Good" is a profound word, something you feel deep in your soul. "Go-o-o-o-o-od!" might be a better translation, good to the bottom of your being.

On the seventh day, God evaluated the whole and declared it "very good" (Gen. 1:31), good multiplied. You and I, in other words, began our career on this planet immersed in God's *very good*-ness. We lived in a wondrous surrounding,that affirmed every part of our being. We ourselves were made in God's image, with the capacity to relate and love as God does (Gen. 1:27).

GO-O-O-O-O-OD!

The best experiences I can remember were the day my wife and I were married and the days when our two children arrived. Life took on a totally different quality. Time didn't matter; an event might take two minutes or an hour and there was no difference. If the sun moved across the sky, I was not aware. A glow of pleasure and profound contentment overlaid everything. Deep down inside, it simply felt "go-o-o-o-o-od!"

The second chapter of Genesis (2:4b-25) tells of Adam and Eve in the goodness of the Garden of Eden. Adam was so happy that he sang a beautiful little song of exhilaration over his wife, Eve, rejoicing in how perfectly they were made for each other: "This . . . is bone of my bones and flesh of my flesh; this one shall be called Woman, for out of Man this one was taken" (Gen. 2:23).

Many readers today are surprised to learn that the creation account in Genesis is actually two different stories placed together: Genesis 1:1–2:4a and Genesis 2:4b-25. Scholars tell us that the latter is clearly older than the former. In the second story, God is immanent, familiar, relating to us as a potter relates to clay, as a parent relates to children walking in a garden. In the first story, God is transcendent, high and lifted up, far above our capacity to comprehend or understand, never at all conversing with us in familiar interchange.

I am convinced that these two creation stories were placed at the beginning of the Bible to give us a full picture of the relationship between human beings and God. God is, on the one hand, our God, close at hand, one who walks with us through the valley of the shadow of death (Ps. 23), one who, if I ascend to heaven or make my bed in sheol, is there with me (Ps. 139). But this same God is, on the other hand, the God of all time and eternity, infinitely greater than I am, never comprehended by me, certainly not one for whom I can ever speak with final authority.

The community that created the Bible wanted us to read it with both pictures in mind. At times we will experience God as near us and with us, supporting us and giving us strength in our endeavors. At other times we will experience God as far beyond us and incomprehensible, having an agenda far larger than ours, doing things we do not understand. As much as we would like to, you and I do not control which experience we will have when.

Immanent theology without transcendent theology becomes spiritual self-centeredness, "just-God-and-me"-ism. American Christian spirituality has been particularly prone to descending into this half-truth. Yet transcendent theology without immanent theology becomes distant and mechanical, conveying that God is "up there somewhere" but not really in touch with us. It is only when we stand these two views of God side by side in all their apparent contradiction, each tugging on and correcting the other, that we are ready to discern the Bible's message.

For the ancient people of God to have begun the Bible with both pictures standing in tandem was absolutely profound, the result of their having lived through both experiences.

FOR DELIBERATION

1. According to William C. Placher, a professor of philosophy and religion at Wabash College in Indiana, "God is not one of the things in the world, to be analyzed and compared with categories appropriate to the other things in the world" (*The Domestication of Transcendence*, p. 10). He believes that much of Christian theology since the seventeenth century has, in its quest to answer unanswerable questions, eliminated Divine Mystery, reducing God to a size we can comprehend. Do you agree with him? Why or why not? Can you think of any examples of this in our culture?

2. Describe experiences in your life that have been "go-o-o-o-o-od!" Is there a certain place that you associate with that feeling?

(Many people say, "My garden.") What could happen in your life that would create "go-o-o-o-o-od!"?

3. According to Genesis 1, words have enormous creative power. God's words created the universe. Our words can create universes too. Remember something someone said to you that has had a huge positive effect in your life. Remember also something someone said that had a huge negative effect in your life. It can work both ways. Think of something you could say to someone else, today or tomorrow, that could have huge creative effect, perhaps to a growing child, to someone striving to achieve something worthwhile, or to someone going through a difficult time.

4. Identify a time in your life when God's immanence, or presence in the world, was critical for you, when the sustaining strength of God carried you through a very difficult situation. Then identify a time when God's transcendence, or unknowable mystery, totally apart from you, opened your eyes to a new perspective you had never seen before.

5

Not So Good

God's very good creation did not last, however. Genesis 3 tells the story of how you and I decided to do things our way. God had told us not to eat from a particular tree in the Garden, but the fruit looked good and a snake talked us into sampling it. Why do we follow snakes?

This initial disobedience was bad enough, but what happened next was worse. When God came to inquire, we refused to take responsibility: "The woman whom you gave to be with me, she gave me fruit from the tree, and I ate" (Gen. 3:12). This was our second (and I think far worse) sin: blaming our wrong on someone else.

This "not-good" element you and I introduced disfigured God's "good" creation. The fields we had cultivated (Gen. 2:15) began to grow weeds and briars as well as wheat (Gen. 3:17). The animals God had placed there as our friends (Gen. 2:18-20a) began biting us (Gen. 3:15). A moment of enormous human exhilaration, childbirth, became infused with excruciating pain (Gen. 3:16). The wonderful, thrilling, marvelous relationship we had enjoyed with each other (Gen. 2:23), our capacity to love one another as God loves (Gen. 1:27-28), came to be diluted with manipulation and exploitation and enmity and strife (Gen. 3:16).

TAKE RESPONSIBILITY FOR YOURSELF

One of the congregations I pastored included three or four clinical psychologists who provided therapy to those struggling with various issues in their lives. From time to time, I would take one of these to lunch and raise the question, "With what are we human beings psychologically sick these days? In what manifestation is our fundamental malady expressing itself?" I almost invariably got the answer, "We spend 95% of our therapy time trying to help people to see how they can take responsibility for their own lives, to stop placing blame on other people or situations and to do what is within *their power* toward *their own* healing." You and I seem to have caught a full dose of Adam's disease.

Nowhere was this more clear than in a doctor's office where I overhead the following conversation:

DOCTOR: You *have to* lose seventy-five pounds.

PATIENT: You'll need to talk to my wife about fixing different food.

DOCTOR: Your wife doesn't need to lose weight. *You* need to lose weight.

PATIENT: Well, yeah, I know, but . . .

We were exiled from our Eden home, turned out to live as fugitives and wanderers on the earth. The door was sealed against our return by two angels bearing flaming swords (Gen. 3:24).

But, lest we think that all was lost and our lives had become destitution, God appeared to help make garments of animal skins to clothe us against the ravages of our exile (Gen. 3:21). We lost the Garden, the home God had prepared, but we did not lose the One who prepared it.

This, then, would be our plight. We would live on an earth that bore the memory of its original goodness, with pleasure and joy and fulfillment all around, but this goodness would now be laced with great struggle. Afflicting forces would set in; pain would become an unending presence. We would find life both a blessing and a curse. God, however, would still show up to help us knit clothes for our survival. We would not be abandoned by our Creator.

As time went on, we would come to perceive that the higher-ups were showing favoritism toward our little brother, Abel, while disdaining us. We were deeply offended at how unfairly we were being treated. And so we imposed our best solution: eliminate Abel. That would solve the problem. We took our little brother into the field and killed him.

The act of violence, however, accomplished far more than we anticipated. It introduced murder into our heritage (Gen. 4:1-16). Violence infected us and refused to go away. We became its servants.

Violence would forever bear this quality: it might accomplish what we intended, but it would also have many other outcomes we did not intend, and it would often accomplish the exact opposite of our intention. We wanted peace in our little family; what we accomplished was to make the spirit of violence spread throughout the human family.

And so a bit later still, when a man struck us, offending our pride, we killed him, instituting vengeance killing in God's creation (Gen. 4:23-24).

Our evil grew until the entire earth became infected: "The Lord saw that the wickedness of humankind was great in the earth, and that every inclination of the thoughts of their hearts was evil continually" (Gen. 6:5). God decided to erase the slate and start over. God sent a flood that covered the earth, allowing just a few of us to escape with our lives, riding out the storm in an ark (Gen. 6-9). But even that measure did not cure. We remained the people we had become.

After the flood, we (Gen. 11:1-9) decided we were weary of being fugitive wanderers on the earth, and we determined that we would build for ourselves a great city to replace the Garden of Eden; we would construct our own security against life's raging. We assembled our highest ingenuity, our best brains, and we began building. We were sure that our city would make us famous, causing the whole world to respect and revere us. As a monument to our greatness, we would build a tower with its top in the heavens, visible throughout the earth.

But the project did not happen as we intended. While executing our plans, our tongues became confused, our words to one another distorted. We were not able to communicate as we needed. We left off building our city and dispersed over the face of the earth. Seeking security, we became insecure. Seeking fame, we became strangers to one another. Seeking respect, we became pitiful. Seeking heaven on our own terms, we created a kind of hell. Thus did our efforts to rebuild Eden conclude.

So ends the opening scene of the Bible's story. God's creation was very good, suited to provide every need. But then we human beings decided we could design a better one on our own, and our willfulness turned it all sour. At scene's end, the creation still embodies its original glory; the world provides enormous fulfillment. But self-centeredness, pretension, jealousy, violence, and destruction have also intruded. It is unclear how God will redeem the wreckage we have made. And yet, God loves us and refuses to withdraw. God's reclamation becomes the subject of the remainder of the book.

I have used the words "we" and "us" through this account because in a very real sense you and I are the human actors in these stories. We are Adam and Eve, who tasted the fruit and tried to evade responsibility for it; we are Cain, whose envy led him to commit murder; we are Lamech, whose desire for vengeance led him, too, to kill; we are Noah, adrift on the ark; we are the people who proposed to build the Tower of Babel. The people who wrote the books of the Bible meant for us to identify with its characters, not just study them from afar. Through the remainder of its story, we will also be Abraham and Sarah, Moses and Deborah, Amos, Mary, Peter and Paul. As our story goes forward, however, I will use only the names of the biblical characters, no longer trying to make obvious the identification between them and us, but no less aware of it.

FOR DELIBERATION

1. Name some area in which you find it difficult to take responsibility for yourself, an area in which you tend to blame your problem on other people or on influences outside your control.

2. Think of a person in whom you see "very good" mixed with "not very good." Jesus told a story about this in Matthew 13:24-30, the parable of the wheat and the tares. He advised his disciples to leave it to God to sort the good from the bad, that they should not take it upon themselves to do so. What do you think Jesus was saying to us in this parable?

3. The writer of Genesis 3:16 apparently found great contradiction in the fact that a moment of exhilarating human joy, the moment of childbirth, is also a moment of excruciating human pain. Similarly, in Genesis 3:17-18, the writer found contradiction in the fact that when a farmer carefully tills the ground and plants seeds, what comes out of the ground is not only wheat, but also weeds and briars. What other instances in human life can you name when success is mingled with failure, ecstasy with agony?

3. An old gospel song contains the line, "Sometimes I feel like a motherless child, a long way from home," echoing Adam and Eve's experience of being ejected from Eden (Gen. 3:23-24). When have you most poignantly felt "a long way from home"?

4. When you felt that way, in the depths of your despair, did God show up to knit garments to keep you warm? What form did that take for you?

5. Why did God accept Abel's offering but reject Cain's? Have you ever known any older brother or sister who understood why those in authority (usually Mom and Dad; in this case, God) so flagrantly favored "that little punk" over him or her?

6. Describe a situation in which you have seen violence grow in a spiral, as it does through these stories (especially in Gen. 4:23-24, in which Cain's murder becomes Lamech's vengeance killing). Jesus (Matt. 18:21-22) asked Peter to set in motion a similar spiral, except with forgiveness rather than violence. Do you know of a situation where faith turned violence into forgiveness? Have you ever seen one act of forgiveness lead to others?

7. Can you think of a situation similar to that in Genesis 11:1-9, in which we human beings set out to build perfection, our own version of the Garden of Eden, and ended up building hell? You might recall that Adolf Hitler's aim was to bring about a perfected, purified humanity. There are many other examples.

6

The Patriarchs

Genesis 12–50 tells the next part of the Bible's story.

God, deciding to take action to reclaim the creation, selected one person, a man named Abram. Abram was no one in particular, just one of the thousands of herders whose flocks of sheep and goats made their way across the grazing lands surrounding the upper Euphrates River. Abram lived with his wife Sarai and their extended family in Haran, a city where the moon was revered as a god.

"Go from your country and your kindred and your father's house to a land that I will show you," God told Abram (Gen. 12:1). Definitive words! Abram was to gather his family and leave Haran and travel southwest into the territory we now call Palestine. ("Palestine" was a name attached many centuries later by the Romans, who named it after an ethnic group who once lived there, the Philistines.)

On his journey, God made three promises to Abram (Gen. 12:1-4): (1) that he would become the father of many descendants, "as many as the stars in the sky or the grains of sand on the seashore"; (2) that God would give him a land to live in, a home that would provide prosperity and security; and (3) that God would bless his family, traveling with them on their trek through history and claiming them as the people of God. Through Abram, God said, all the families of

GO FROM YOUR COUNTRY AND YOUR KINDRED AND YOUR FATHER'S HOUSE. . . .

The child paused before entering the red brick building. In one hand he carried a metal lunch box not yet scarred by use. In the other hand he carried a binder with seven carefully sharpened pencils and two first grade tablets. He had anticipated this moment for days, arranging and rearranging his school supplies to discover the best possible order, asking questions of those who had been there before about what to expect, wearing his older brother's backpack to pretend that he, too, was a school veteran. And now his time had come. It was no longer an exciting game about growing up. He wondered what would happen. Would he get lost, unable to find his way through the masses of unfamiliar faces and down the long halls that led to places where he had never been? Would he do something wrong and incur the wrath of higher powers who might be watching? No mother to set right his mistakes now. No father to turn to for safety. Only one six-year-old in a world of strangers. A foreboding place, the first grade. He moved through the school door, taking his first tentative steps toward adulthood.

"Go from your country and your kindred and your father's house. . . ." This call is spoken to us all repeatedly through life. Time and again, we are called to leave home and migrate into a strange country. Every moment beckons us from a secure present into an insecure future. There is no choice; we are forever on our way.

the earth would be blessed — this was God's plan to redeem the creation.

Descendants, land, blessing: God's promises. These promises formed *God's covenant with Abram.*

This covenant would become the cornerstone of the biblical story.

Abram and Sarai, renamed Abraham and Sarah as part of the covenant, would become the father and mother of Israel: every Israelite would count his or her lineage beginning at this moment, and so throughout their history, the people of Israel would say, "We are children of Abraham." God's covenant with Abraham and Sarah would become a covenant with all Israel through all time. The promises of descendants, land, and blessing would stand as the defining articles of Israelite faith.

Abraham and his family, we are told in Genesis 12:4a, obeyed God's bidding. They traveled southward and took up residence in Palestine. More than a thousand years later, the author of the New Testament book of Hebrews would write, "By faith Abraham obeyed

. . . .To a Land That I Will Show You

Several years ago I stood in a hospital room with a dying friend, a knowledgeable and experienced pastor. He had received news only two hours before that his illness was terminal, and he was, needless to say, profoundly shaken. I went in wondering what I would say. My friend was a very bright man, and I knew it was not the time for anything trite — he had heard it all before. What I spoke would need to be genuine. After brief opening greetings, he said, "Well, Jim, according to the doctor, I'm dying. Do you have anything you can say to me?"

Usually I am not good at coming up with the right words on-the-spot like that. But on this day, God spoke through me. "The Lord said to Abraham and Sarah, 'Go from your country and your kindred and your father's house to a land that I will show you.'"

He brightened. "I guess that's it, isn't it?" he said. "That is the point."

Yes, I think that is the point.

when he was called to set out for a place that he was to receive as an inheritance; and he set out, not knowing where he was going" (Heb. 11:8). Abraham's faith in embarking on this journey would be honored and respected in Israel through all generations.

Yet it was not long before the people God had chosen to work with began to reveal their true colors (Gen. 12:10-20). A famine broke out in Palestine, and eventually starvation threatened Abraham and Sarah. So they traveled southward toward Egypt seeking food. As they neared Egypt, however, Abraham realized that he faced a serious problem. His wife Sarah was beautiful to behold, and Pharaoh, the Egyptian king, had a reputation for taking just such women into his harem. The king would order Abraham killed so that he could seize Sarah.

So Abraham said to Sarah, "Let's tell them you're my sister; then even if Pharaoh takes a liking to you, they won't kill me." It was a rotten plot, but Sarah complied. Pharaoh did indeed take her into his harem, and in exchange offered Abraham a very large gift of livestock. The family hunger problem was solved.

But God was not happy in the least! God rained affliction on Pharaoh until Pharaoh finally realized what was going on. He returned Sarah to Abraham, along with a royal admonishment for the deceit and an invitation to leave Egypt at his earliest convenience.

This story establishes clearly the sort of people God had to work with in redeeming the creation. "The chosen" possessed no particular claim on moral virtue. They did not become lights of purity. They were quite ordinary human beings. Thus we begin to see that creation would be redeemed not by human virtue but by God's character, God's persistence, God's grace.

Abraham and Sarah went back to Palestine with all the livestock they had received from Pharaoh. For a while, things went well for them. But over time, an enormous problem began to emerge: Sarah was barren. She bore no offspring. How could she and Abraham become the parents of a multitude if they had no children? God repeated the covenant promise several times — "I will make you the father of a great nation" — but Sarah did not conceive a child. For years, decades, nothing happened. Finally, when Sarah was ninety years old and Abra-

MIRRORS FOR OUR IDENTITY

The spectacle of Pharaoh's lecturing Father Abraham on ethics is formidable! It is entirely possible that the heathen will be more righteous than the saint, the lost more honorable than the found. This dynamic recurs across the biblical story. Being God's chosen people, the church, is no assurance of moral virtue.

"The Bible does not show us models for our morality but mirrors for our identity," biblical scholar James Sanders has said many times. The Bible's human figures are not the people we *should be* but the people we *are*. Genesis is not telling us to be like Abraham; it is telling us that Abraham is like us: very faithful and devout at times and very insecure and self-centered at other times. That, the Bible understands, is who God has to work with.

ham one hundred, an angel visited them (Gen. 18), under the guise of a stranger traveling down the road, to tell them that Sarah was about to become pregnant. At the news, Sarah and Abraham both laughed, heartily and aloud, thinking this was absurd. But, despite their doubt, ninety-year-old Sarah did conceive, and nine months later gave birth to a son, Isaac. The faithfulness of God prevailed.

This became a very large, recurring theme in Israel's story: human certainty that God's promise was doomed, and God's faithfulness in fulfilling the promise nevertheless. It would happen in ways no one expected.

This whole story of Abraham and Sarah, and of God's covenant with them, is found in Genesis 12–24.

Abraham and Sarah's son Isaac became the patriarch of the next generation. His story is told in Genesis 25–26.

Isaac and his wife Rebekah bore twin sons, Esau and Jacob. Jacob, the younger of the two, spent nearly his entire life plotting to gain the upper hand (Gen. 27–36). Jacob would manipulate any situation to get his wish. He tricked his father Isaac, tricked his elder brother Esau, tricked his uncle Laban, and even attempted to strike favorable deals with God. As Jacob grew older, God changed his name to Israel, "the one who strives with God." The nation to be born from Abraham was given the name Israel to acknowledge that it bore the same basic character as Jacob.

Jacob, his two wives, Rachel and Leah, and their two handmaids,

THE GOSPEL AS COMEDY

Writer and Presbyterian minister Frederick Buechner offers a striking description of Sarah and Abraham hearing the news about their soon-to-be-born son:

"The place to start is with a woman laughing. She is an old woman, and, after a lifetime in the desert, her face is cracked and rutted like a six-month drought. She hunches her shoulders around her ears and starts to shake. She squinnies her eyes shut, and her laughter is still all china teeth and wheeze and tears running down as she rocks back and forth in the kitchen chair. She is laughing because she is pushing ninety-one hard and has just been told that she is going to have a baby. Even though it was an angel who told her, she can't control herself, and her husband can't control himself either. He keeps a straight face a few seconds longer than she does, but he ends by cracking up, too. . . .

"The old woman's name is Sarah, of course, and the old man's name is Abraham, and they are laughing at the idea of a baby's being born in the geriatric ward and Medicare's picking up the tab." (*Telling the Truth: The Gospel as Tragedy, Comedy, and Fairy Tale,* pp. 49-50)

JOSEPH AND JESUS

At the beginning of the Joseph story, as difficult things were happening between Joseph and his brothers, the Genesis writer says, "[Joseph's] father kept the matter in mind" (Gen. 37:11b).

At the beginning of Luke's version of the Jesus story, as unusual things were happening with angels and shepherds, Luke says that "Mary treasured all these words and pondered them in her heart" (Luke 2:19, repeated in 2:51).

These two are essential equivalents, Luke's version of a "footnote." Luke was saying that if we want to understand what God was doing through Jesus, we need to recall what God did through Joseph.

When Jesus was deserted by his brothers (the disciples) and sold for thirty pieces of silver, God used this evil to redeem those who had committed it, just as God had so many years earlier used the evil deeds committed by Joseph's brother to work their redemption.

God's ways are wondrous and magnificent!

Bilhah and Zilpah, produced twelve sons. Joseph (Gen. 37, 39–50), the next-to-youngest, was hated by his older brothers. Not only did father Jacob love him most, but bratty little Joseph insisted on lording this fact over his brothers, proclaiming that they would grow up to be his servants. The older brothers could take only so much of this, and one day while they were in the field grazing the family flock, they decided to take care of things once and for all. Some slave traders came by in their wagon, and his brothers sold Joseph into slavery for twenty pieces of silver! The traders went on their way, and eventually sold Joseph to a government official in Egypt.

In Egypt, Joseph had an eventful, up-and-down life, at times doing exceedingly well and at other times landing in prison. When his brothers, a number of years later, experienced famine up in Palestine and had to travel into Egypt to survive, they found that their little brother Joseph had been highly successful and had risen to become Pharaoh's minister of agriculture. The family was given food because their brother Joseph was in charge. God, in other words, quietly and imperceptibly, had used the hatred of ten brothers for their sibling to save them all from starvation. "You meant evil against me; but God meant it for good, to bring it about that many people should be kept alive, as they are today" (Gen. 50:20, RSV). Such, the Bible says, are the wondrous and magnificent ways of the Almighty.

The Patriarchs — Abraham, Isaac, and Jacob — were exactly that, fathers of Israel. In each generation, God's promise to Abraham — descendants, land, and blessing — faced formidable obstacles, but remained intact. This is the fundamental pattern running through Genesis 12–50: God's promise, human obstacles to that promise, and God's faithfulness to it. We end the patriarchal period with Israel in Egypt, well fed and royally treated. The opening of the next era in Israel's story will not be nearly as happy.

FOR DELIBERATION

1. Describe a situation in which you, or someone close to you, has been told, "Go from your country and your kindred and your father's house to a land that I will show you" (Gen. 12:1). What regrets do we human beings have at those times? What apprehensions about the future? What hopes?

2. Does the Bible's picture of Abraham, as profoundly faithful in one moment and fearfully self-centered in the next, describe you in any way? When have you alternated between faithfulness and fear?

3. Discuss James Sanders's statement, "The Bible does not show us models for our morality but mirrors for our identity." What will this mean as we teach Bible stories to children?

4. Do you know people like Jacob (Gen 27–36) — bright, scheming people who spend a lifetime conniving to get what they want,

even trying to wrestle a blessing from God, yet through whom God seems to be at work?

5. Jacob is given a new name, Israel (Gen. 32:28). What is the writer of this story saying by having the nation of Abraham's descendants, Israel, named after Jacob?

6. What would you name as the major barriers for the church in setting aside anti-Semitism? How do you think Christians should think of and relate to Jews?

7. Describe a situation in which you have seen God take the evil in human hearts and bring from it good and blessing for people. What are the dangers of believing that God does that?

7

Exodus and Wilderness

Exodus, the second book of the Bible, begins with Israel in Egypt. Generations had passed since the time of the Patriarchs, and Egypt's pharaohs had no memory of Joseph and his brothers. The people of Israel had gone from being honored guests to exploited slaves, brick makers in the service of the pharaohs' massive building projects up and down the Nile River. They were treated harshly, required to work long days of hard labor for little return. If they complained, their burdens were increased. Their taskmasters regarded them as inferior, good-for-nothing people, at the bottom of society's ladder. But they were also feared because they were prolific. Despite their maltreatment, they grew in strength, size, and numbers.

God appeared one day in a burning bush to one of the Israelites, Moses, while he was tending sheep (Exod. 3). God told Moses that he was to go before Pharaoh and declare that he was to let Israel go free, that Israel had been praying to the God of their ancestors and that their God was answering them. God further specified that Moses, at that point an obscure shepherd, was to lead Israel out of Egypt under divine direction.

Moses was astounded! "Why me? Pharaoh won't take me seriously! Israel won't believe me! I'm not a good enough speaker or

> **ARE YOU KIDDING?**
>
> Imagine if a Chicago sanitation worker walked into the mayor's office one day to announce that his God had told him that all the city's garbage collectors were to leave their work and gather in the Arizona desert for a month of worship and celebration . . . and that the mayor was to pay their way there and back! Such was the audacity of Moses' request to Pharaoh.

leader! I don't even know you that well, God; I'm not that religious! Find someone else!" God listened patiently to all of Moses' objections and then replied quite simply, "Go!" Moses went.

Not surprisingly, Pharaoh was of no mind to free his slaves. He paid no heed. God, therefore, sent massive plagues on Egypt (Exod. 7:14–12:32): frogs, gnats, flies, diseases, and the like. But Pharaoh's heart remained hardened. The final plague was the death of all firstborn sons throughout the land of Egypt, killed by an angel sent by God one night. The angel "passed over" Israel's firstborn, an act commemorated to this day on the feast day of Passover.

After this awful event, the Egyptians urged Israel to leave the land, fearing that otherwise they would all soon die (Exod. 12:33). With Moses leading the migration, Israel journeyed eastward toward the Red Sea, beyond which they would pass out of Egypt into the Sinai Peninsula. God traveled with them on this journey, leading them in the form of a cloud by day and a pillar of fire by night (Exod. 13:21). At the Red Sea, however, Israel halted, unsure how to cross over. The waters were deep, and there was no boat or bridge.

By this time, Pharaoh's mind had changed (Exod. 14:5). Slaves were too valuable to Egypt's economy to set free. Pharaoh sent his army to pursue them. With the army bearing down from the rear, Israel could feel the savagery and destruction that was about to happen.

But a great marvel occurred. A wind arose (in the Hebrew language, "wind" and "spirit" are the same word, so the Hebrews would certainly have sensed God at work in this) and parted the waters of the sea, creating a dry pathway from shore to shore. Israel moved along the pathway, walking on dry ground. From one side to the other they traveled until all were safe (Exod. 14:21-22). But when Pharaoh's army tried to follow, the wheels of their chariots mired in the mud and the waters flowed back together. The army drowned (Exod. 14:23-29). Thus was Israel saved from certain slaughter and return to captivity. God reached forth with a mighty hand and outstretched arm to set them free.

It was to become the defining moment in the history of this people. Formerly, they had been nothing, slaves, unnoticed by history, of zero importance on the human stage. Now, God had listened to them, saved them, claimed them. God would many times after this answer the prayers of those in acute need by attending to their desperate

GOD'S GONNA TROUBLE THE WATER

In the American South before the Civil War, bloodhounds on the trail of a runaway slave could track that slave right up to the edge of the creek or stream, but no farther. Once the slave got into the water, the scent was washed away. This is reflected in the old spiritual:

Wade in the water,
Wade in the water, children,
Wade in the water,
God's gonna trouble the water,
God's gonna trouble the water.

"Wade in the Water" was sung at baptisms. But embedded in the song was a hidden meaning: the water washes away not only sin but scent. Get into the water and travel there! God will send miracles of deliverance, just as God sent the great miracle to the children of Israel!

plight with a saving love (Psalm 107). God would become known not as one who supports kings and princes in their exercise of power but as one who regards the earth's wretched and redeems them. This attribute would be revealed as a primary characteristic of God: God's inclination for taking a tiny seed and turning it into a great plant, for taking death and breathing into it life.

This wondrous event — when God commanded the waters of the sea to obey in delivering God's people from slavery — would be remembered and celebrated through all generations in the family of Abraham!

After dancing and singing on the eastern shore of the Red Sea (Exod. 15:1-21), Israel began a journey through the Sinai Peninsula toward Palestine, the Promised Land, the home of their ancestors Abraham, Isaac, and Jacob. The Bible says that their journey across Sinai took forty years, a lengthy period for covering, at most, four hundred miles. But in the Bible the number forty represents *a time of preparation*, a time of getting ready for what is to happen next (see "Numbers" sidebar, page 64). In this case, God was preparing them for life in the Promised Land under the One who had saved them at the Red Sea.

No sooner had they set out into Sinai, however, than things went wrong (Exod. 15:22ff.). They became thirsty, then hungry. No water, no food. They complained! Why had Moses brought them out into this desert? Didn't Moses and his God even have a plan to provide their daily fare? They may have been slaves in Egypt, but at least they had food there! Had they come out here to die?

Of course, God had not brought them to the desert to die. God found water holes for them to drink from, sent quail and a food called manna from heaven for them to eat, provided for their needs. But their grumbling continued. They complained, it turned out, not because they had anything serious to complain about, but because they were a complaining people, self-absorbed, stubborn and stiff-necked. Their trek through Sinai would unveil the full measure of their complaining spirit, which became so wearying at times that God threatened to abandon the entire venture.

DISCONTENT

The following are comments I, a pastor, have received over the years on how to improve worship:

You look better when you don't lean forward on the pulpit . . . I don't like seeing the choir's feet . . . The heat is up too high . . . The air conditioning is down too low . . . The pew cushions are getting lumpy . . . The bulletin print is too soft . . . The music is too loud . . . The prayers are too long . . . The traffic noise outside is too distracting . . . I don't like green choir robes . . . The hymns are all that new stuff . . . The hymns are all that old stuff . . . I've never liked Easter lilies . . .

God's people haven't changed much, have we?

The Hebrews traveled to Mt. Sinai (whose location is uncertain to us today, although there is a likely candidate in the southern Sinai Peninsula). There (Exod. 19), they encamped at the base while Moses climbed to the summit to talk with God. Over the next forty days, God spoke to Moses through a thick darkness, and the Bible describes God's voice as being like thunder and lightning, or the sound of a trumpet (Exod. 20:18-21). Moses received instructions on how Israel was to live after they entered the Promised Land. The instructions consisted of two parts: the Ten Commandments (Exod. 20:1-17) and the covenant code (Exod. 20:22–23:33).

But no sooner did Moses descend from Mt. Sinai than he found Israel in turmoil. The people had grown frightened in his absence, and had decided they needed to fashion their own god, a golden bull they could see and trust (Exod. 32–34). So they melted all their gold jewelry together, made such a god, and threw a wild party to celebrate how *it* had brought them out of Egypt (Exod. 32:6)! Seeing it, Moses' anger burned! God's anger burned far hotter. God threatened to annihilate Israel on the spot, to kill them all. Many died that day. The anger of God was fearsome! But Moses pleaded with God to remember

45

APODICTIC AND CASUISTIC LAW

The covenant code is "casuistic law"; that is, for each transgression, there is a stipulated punishment: "If someone does *x*, the penalty shall be *y*." The effort is made to cover multiple circumstances in the nation's life.

The Ten Commandments, on the other hand, are "apodictic law": "You shall . . . ; you shall not . . . !" There is no punishment stipulated; these are simply things the community *is to do!* Worship no other gods before God, use the sacred gift of language with integrity rather than with deceit, honor God's time (the Sabbath), honor parents and family, honoring the sanctity of human life, not commit adultery, not steal, not bear false witness about other people, not be greedy — these were ethical cornerstones, eternal laws that were valid in every circumstance. For the community to follow them would lead to life; for the community to transgress them would lead to sure and certain death.

the promise made to Abraham long ago, and God repented, finally agreeing to renew the covenant.

The golden calf episode was one of the sorriest incidents in Israel's life. Here was another glimpse at the darker side of the chosen. "Stubborn and stiff-necked," as Moses called this people (Exod. 34:9), was only too accurate. For all their occasional virtue and faith, God's elect were self-centered, insecure, self-protective, and rebellious. We have to thank God for not abandoning the challenge.

Following a blueprint God had specified (Exod. 27–31), Israel constructed a tabernacle for God (Exod. 35–40). The tabernacle was a large portable tent that housed the ark of the covenant. The ark was a large, empty wooden chest meant to serve as the vehicle God would occupy as Israel traveled through the Sinai wilderness. Of course, no one would ever mistake an empty wooden box for God, thinking it an image to be worshipped. But the ark did provide the focal point of God's traveling presence amid the people. When the construction was finished, "[a] cloud covered the tent . . . , and the glory of the Lord filled the tabernacle. Moses was not able to enter the tent . . . because the cloud settled upon it, and the glory of the Lord filled the tabernacle" (Exod. 40:34-35). The cloud became Israel's traveling guide on the journey to the Promised Land. Wherever the cloud went, Israel went.

God also stipulated through Moses the many purification and

THE JUBILEE

One of the most important and innovative ideas in Israelite law was the Jubilee, laid out in Leviticus 25. The Jubilee was an observance to be celebrated in Israel every fiftieth year. After seven cycles of seven years, the fiftieth year was to be a year of release throughout the land. All slaves were to be set free. All prisoners were to be released. All lands that had been sold and bought were to return to their original owners. Any servitude, any indebtedness, was to be forgiven. Farmers were to give the land a year of rest and live off the bounty of previous years.

The Jubilee was meant to be a recurring return to the Exodus, to the time when God's grace had poured out upon a lowly, oppressed people to give them the vitality of new life. It was to be marked by a great celebration, especially among the lowly and the oppressed, giving thanks for God's continuing grace.

The Jubilee, as a deep and fervent hope, would over the course of the centuries help Israel to believe even through their worst enslavements and ordeals that God would act to deliver them. Especially during years when the nation was gripped tightly in the controlling fist of a foreign tyrant, the Jubilee was their great hope.

CANAANITE BAAL WORSHIP

The Baal worship of the Canaanites would prove repeatedly to be a major temptation for Israel. It is easy to see why.

The Canaanites were agricultural people who grew their food in the fields. A large part of their religion was to encourage their gods to make the fields productive. In the Canaanite concept of the universe, the earth was female. To grow food, female Earth needed to be fertilized by the male god in the sky, Baal. Rain was understood as Baal's having sexual intercourse with female Earth.

Baal, however, tended to be forgetful and to lose interest. The result was drought. To end drought, or to prevent it, the Canaanites engaged in ritual prostitution, human females and males keeping Baal reminded of what he was supposed to do. Israel was highly tempted by this worship because they, too, depended on the rain that was often so scarce.

The God of the Bible stands in stark contrast, refusing to be manipulated by human beings. No amount of ritual incantation — and certainly no ritual prostitution! — could cajole God into bending to human purpose. The biblical question was never, "Can we convince God to do what we want?" It was, "Can God convince us to do what God wants?" There is a world of difference!

worship rituals Israel was to follow in their new home, and these are found in the Book of Leviticus.

And, finally, God set forth how the twelve tribes of Israel, the descendants of the sons of Jacob, were to proceed in formation surrounding the tabernacle (Num. 1–2). The tribes of Reuben, Simeon, Judah, Issachar, Zebulun, Ephraim, Manasseh, Benjamin, Dan, Asher, Gad, and Naphtali would, for the next five hundred years, constitute the nation Israel.

AROUND THE WORLD

The Exodus from Egypt and the trek through Sinai very likely happened in the thirteenth century B.C.E.

In the same century, history's first books were being made in China.

Ramses II, the Egyptian pharaoh, was erecting a colossal statue of himself at Memphis, as well as copy versions all over his domain (one currently stands in Memphis, Tennessee). He was also building a magnificent temple at Luxor.

According to legend the Trojan War, brought on by the abduction of Helen by Paris, and completed when Greece destroyed Troy, took place in this century.

Israel set out on their long journey across Sinai (Num. 10:11). Their complaints against God continued (Num. 11:1-15). They sent spies to scout out the Promised Land, which was at that time occupied by Canaanites, and the spies reported back that the Canaanites were giants. This word created panic among them (Num. 13–14). A rebellion within Israel's ranks challenged Moses' leadership (Num. 16). At Meribah, the people complained even more harshly because they were thirsty, until God brought water from a rock (Num. 20:1-13). Israel sought to travel through the territory of Edom, but a large Edomite force prohibited their passage (Num. 20:14-21). Taking another more difficult route, they had to battle the armies of Sihon and Og, two local kings (Num. 21:21-35).

Finally arriving in the plains of Moab on the eastern shore of the Jordan River, Israel set up camp for an extended period to prepare for its conquest of the Promised Land. The sheer number of Israelites who had descended on his land made Balak, the king of Moab, deeply afraid. So he hired Balaam, a local seer, to place a curse on Israel. But when Balaam opened his mouth to speak the curse, out came a blessing (Num. 22–24). As Israel settled in at Moab, a number of Israelite men began engaging in ritual sex with Moabite women at shrines of the Canaanite god Baal. God's wrath burned so mightily against them that twenty-four thousand died (Num. 25).

In all, the journey from Mt. Sinai to the Promised Land was harsh and difficult. The people of Israel repeatedly showed their most complaining and rebellious side. But God, despite much anger, traveled in Israel's midst to provide passage. The main point of the Exodus and wilderness story is to proclaim the unfathomable, incomprehensible, incredible, unending faithfulness of God. Once God makes a promise, God does not give it up, no matter what!

For Deliberation

1. God did not appear in Egypt to consult with Pharaoh on how to rule, but instead to consult with Pharaoh's slaves on how to escape. What does this say about God? How does it shape the rest of the Bible? What does it mean for Christian faith? What difference is it to make in the way Christian believers live?

2. If you had been Pharaoh, what would have gone through your mind at Moses' request?

3. On the other hand, if you had been a Hebrew brickmaker in Pharaoh's labor corps, what would have gone through your mind when a sheepherder you had never seen before stood among your people and announced that God wanted you to flee into the hot, dry wasteland of the Sinai Desert and find your freedom there?

4. Why do you think God continues to put up with a people as complaining, as anxious, as self-consumed, as we are?

5. If God were defining "ethical cornerstones," apodictic laws for good and faithful life in our country today, what do you think God's list would include? How do you think the laws God would give today would be the same as, or different from, the Ten Commandments given over 3,000 years ago? Note: projecting what God would say is high-hazard business. We all need humility, and no one should ever be too sure of being right. And yet, the church, the believing community, is charged with carrying on this

deliberation always, bringing God's meaning behind the ancient command into the modern day. Don't answer this question by yourself. That answer will reflect only your narrow viewpoint. Discuss it in *a diverse group,* feeding and limiting one another, and arriving at the best consensus possible.

6. If you were writing an essay on how you, and the people you identify with most closely, are "stubborn and stiff-necked" people (Exod. 34:9), what would you say? That is, if you were composing a prayer of confession that confesses the sin of *you and your type of folks,* what would that prayer say? It is easy, and useless, to confess other people's sin; it is challenging, difficult, and ultimately much more worthwhile to confess our own sin.

7. When I was a child, I somehow believed that "the glory of the Lord" dwelled in the chancel of my church's worship sanctuary, and that I should treat that space with great reverence. Did you ever have that feeling? Do you have a *sacred place* in your life now, a special location that surrounds you with awe and wonder? If not, are there times when you wish you did? For many Christians, the communion table is one of those places.

8. Where has the ancient jubilee tradition found expression in our world today? Do you remember Jubilee 2000?

9. One modern commentator has called much of today's religion "lobbying for special favors in the courts of the Almighty." Identify ways in which you think we try to manipulate and coerce God into doing what we want, as Baal worshippers did 3,000 years ago.

8

The Promised Land

In the plains of Moab, on the east bank of the Jordan River, Israel prepared to enter the Promised Land. As they made ready, Moses preached a sermon on how they were to live after they occupied the land. The sermon was unduly long, as many are, but powerfully stated. Today, we know it as the Book of Deuteronomy.

The sermon began (Deut. 6:4-9) by asserting that the greatest imperative for Israel was to love their God with all their heart and all their soul and all their might. Beyond all the laws, all the rules, all the guidelines, all the regulations, this was the critical factor for the survival of their community: love. It was to be Israel's response to the immense love God had shown them in freeing them from bondage in Egypt and leading them through the great and terrible wilderness with its scorpions and fiery serpents and endless conflicts. Israel was to tell the story of this deliverance to their children through all generations, and to arouse in their children this same love for God.

Moses went on to tell Israel (Deut. 8) that, after their generations of slavery in Egypt, after their years of struggle in the desert, they were about to become exceedingly rich, that the land they were crossing the Jordan to possess flowed with streams of water, grew food in abundance, and prolifically yielded ores from the ground. Moses warned the people sternly, strongly, that their newfound richness must not puff up their heads and harden their hearts: "Do not say to yourself, 'My power and the might of my own hand have gotten me this wealth.'" In other words, do not think you have become rich because of any special virtue in you. Do not become arrogant, believing yourselves to be superior to others who have less than you have. It is God who is giving you this wealth, not because you deserve it, but because God promised it, because God loves you. Deuteronomy 8 remains to this day a resounding admonition against the haughty complacency that can easily afflict us when we become prosperous.

Moses continued, "If there is among you anyone in need, a member of your community . . . , do not be hard-hearted or tight-fisted toward your needy neighbor. . . . Rather, open your hand, willingly lending enough to meet the need, whatever it may be. Be careful that you do not entertain a mean thought. . . . Give liberally and be ungrudging" (Deut. 15:7-11).

Moses spoke special words to Israel's future king, telling him that he was to make for himself a handwritten copy of God's instruction (this same Book of Deuteronomy) and read it day and night, that he was not ever, because of his great power, to consider himself above the law. The king was to be the most law-abiding citizen in the entire land, shunning any notion of executive privilege (Deut. 17:14-20)! He was to lead the nation in doing what was right! For as the king acted, so would the people follow.

The underlying point of Moses' sermon was that, just as God was giving Israel this land, God could also take it from them. Just as they were being made exceedingly rich by God's grace, they could be made woefully destitute by God's judgment. To avoid that plight, Israel was to take God's will into the depths of their hearts and follow it. "Keep these words that I am commanding you today in your heart. Recite them to your children and talk about them when you are at home and when you are away, when you lie down and when you rise. Bind them as a sign on your hand, fix them as an emblem on your forehead, and write them on the doorpost of your house and of your gates" (Deut. 6:6-9).

Moses spoke a final blessing on his beloved people, Israel (Deut. 33), and died (Deut. 34). He was buried in a valley in Moab. The place of his burial was kept secret, lest subsequent generations try to go there to worship him as a god. Deuteronomy ends with the words, "Never since has there arisen a prophet in Israel like Moses, whom the Lord knew face to face."

No moment in Israel's life has inspired more creativity, more imagination, more rich imagery, than this moment on the eastern bank of the Jordan River. God's people, after generations of slavery in Egypt, after years of travel through a treacherous and difficult wilderness, were ready to cross the river and possess God's rich gift. From struggle to abundance! From difficulty to joy! From oppression to freedom! From obscurity to renown! From death to life! Christians to this day maintain the same hope.

God named Joshua to take up the leadership of Israel, and it was he who led the people in their conquest of Canaan. Joshua's first act was to send spies across the river to the city of Jericho to scout out the land. A Jericho prostitute named Rahab took in the spies and kept them from being found by the king. In return, Rahab and her family were spared when Israel invaded the land (Josh. 2).

With due ritual and fanfare, Israel passed over the Jordan River into the Promised Land. God held back the waters of the Jordan just as God had parted the waters of the Red Sea, so that the people passed through on dry ground. Twelve rocks were piled up in the river as a memorial to their crossing. The memorial was called, in Hebrew, an *ebenezer.*

At the blast of seven trumpets, Joshua defeated Jericho in one of the most famous conflicts in the Bible (Josh. 6). After that, deception helped him to defeat the city of Ai (Josh. 8:1-29). From Ai he and his men went on to defeat numerous other kings north and south, until the Promised Land was settled by Israel. The stories of these conquests are filled with passion, intrigue, trickery, and, most of all, victory (Josh. 9–11). God's faithfulness in giving the land remained firm. A full list of kings conquered by Moses and by Joshua is recorded in Joshua 12.

GOING OVER JORDAN

Christians have adopted the image of the Israelites crossing Jordan to give expression to the hope of being united with Jesus and with departed loved ones in the next life, as in the case of this beloved old hymn.

The Wayfaring Stranger

I am a poor wayfaring stranger,
    While traveling thro' this world below
There is no sickness, toil, nor danger
    In that bright land to which I go.
I going there to meet my father,
    I'm going there no more to roam;
I am just going over Jordan,
    I am just going over home.

I know dark clouds will gather o'er me,
    I know my pathway's rough and steep;
But golden fields lie out before me,
    Where weary eyes no more shall weep.
I'm going there to meet my mother,
    She said she'd meet me when I come;
I am just going over Jordan,
    I am just going over home.

I'll soon be free from every trial,
    This form will rest beneath the sod;
I'll drop the cross of self-denial,
    And enter in my home with God.
I'm going there to see my Savior,
    Who shed for me His precious blood;
I am just going over Jordan,
    I am just going over home.

With the territory occupied, God allotted portions of the Promised Land to each of the twelve tribes of Israel (Josh. 13–19). Reuben was given a plot, Simeon a plot, Judah a plot, Dan a plot, and so on down the line. Each tribe took up residence on its land.

The Bible does not describe the particulars, but it seems that each family within each tribe was given a portion of the tribe's territory, so that every Israelite family received from God a land-gift. This land-gift was called an "inheritance." Because God had given it, the inheritance was not subject to human transactions — buying and selling; it was to remain in the family through all generations. The inheritance became a sacred entity. The people were not to transgress God's stipulations by engaging in real estate transactions. Inheritance, both the phenomenon and the concept, would play a key role in the nation's future.

With the land distributed, Joshua "gathered all the tribes of Israel to Shechem" (Josh. 24:1) and led a covenant renewal ceremony, reviewing for the people the history of God's relationship with them, beginning with Abraham (Josh. 24:2-13). He then called upon the people steadfastly to serve the God who had brought them successfully through this perilous and difficult path, not the fertility gods of the Canaanites they would encounter in the Promised Land.

Joshua spoke to Israel the well-known and oft-quoted words, "Now if you are unwilling to serve the LORD, choose this day whom you will serve, whether the gods your ancestors served in the region beyond the River or the gods of the Amorites [Canaanites] in whose

EBENEZER

"Here I raise my ebenezer; Hither by Thy help I come," sings the second verse of the famous hymn, "Come, Thou Fount of Every Blessing." Frequent church worshipers have asked, "What is an ebenezer?" It is a memorial pile of rocks, literally, stones of succor or aid.

land you are living; but as for me and my household, we will serve the Lord" (Josh. 24:15).

For Deliberation

1. Why do you think prosperity goes to our heads so easily? Why, when God blesses us greatly, do we so readily get haughty and arrogant? How can great blessing make us humble and thankful instead of arrogant?

2. Do you agree with Moses that the king, or president, or other ruler, of a nation should have to live under the same laws as everyone else, or should the leader enjoy special privileges? If so, what should those privileges cover?

3. List as many historical instances as you can in which "crossing the Jordan" imagery has been used to interpret events. Where might you apply this imagery in your life?

4. God, the Book of Joshua says, gave each Israelite tribe and each Israelite family an "inheritance," a piece of land that was to be their home through the generations. "Home" is a sacred idea, a deeply meaningful concept. In one of my classes, someone said, "Home is where no matter how big you get, they know how small you are, and no matter how small you get, they know how big you are." See if you can do that well with other statements. How would you describe home?

9

Era of the Judges

It is impossible to date events accurately this early in the Bible's story, but it seems that for the better part of two hundred years after the conquest of Canaan, the people of Israel lived a rural life. No large cities appeared, only small villages. No central religious site was established, only local shrines. No regular army was formed, only impromptu fighting units. No national leadership developed, only local elders and judges. No central institutions drew the nation together. It was an era of dispersed living, of local autonomy, with each tribe and each family occupying its own inheritance, growing its own food, populating its own territory, protecting its own borders. This is the time period we read about in the Book of Judges.

Throughout the Book of Judges, the other small kingdoms surrounding Israel waged attacks on it: Aram (Judges 3:7-11), Moab (Judges 3:12-30), Canaan (Judges 4–5), Midian (Judges 6–8), Ammon (Judges 10:6–11:33), the Philistines (Judges 13–15). The stories of these attacks follow a consistent pattern: Israel sinned against God, usually by worshipping Baal or one of the other gods of the region. God gave them into the hands of a neighboring kingdom, which defeated them and ruled them for a time. Suffering under the yoke of their oppressors, Israel cried to God for help. God heard their cries and raised from their ranks a strong and powerful "judge." This judge was a charismatic leader who rallied an Israelite force and drove out the oppressor. Peace and well-being were restored to the Promised Land. In this pattern, God called a succession of judges: Othniel, Ehud, Deborah, Gideon, Jephthah, and Samson, each to deliver Israel.

Three of these judges are particularly notable. Deborah (Judges 4–5), a prophetess, summoned an Israelite named Barak to gather a fighting force to drive out the army of the Canaanites, which had conquered a territory in northern Israel two decades earlier. The Canaanites were under the leadership of Sisera, chief military commander for King Jabin. With Deborah present to invoke the Lord's spirit, not only did Barak's men annihilate Sisera's army, but they caused Sisera himself to flee alone on foot. Exhausted after running a long distance, Sisera sought refuge in the tent of a woman named Jael, only to have Jael drive a tent peg through his temple as he slept. Deborah and Barak joined in a victory song now found in Judges 5, a song that celebrates the wondrous and unpredictable ways in which God works to deliver Israel from its oppressors.

Forty years passed, and the nearby kingdom of Midian began to trouble Israel. So God called a man named Gideon (Judges 6–8). Gideon, with a force of only three hundred fighting men, threw the huge army of the Midianites, a hundred times its size, into a nighttime panic by blowing trumpets, smashing jars, and shouting from the hilltops surrounding Midian's encampment. In terror, the Midianites turned on one another, more dying by their own swords than by the swords of Israel. Gideon led Israel into another forty years of peace.

REMINDERS FOR TRAVELERS

Travelers today have two reminders of the era of the judges. The Samsonite brand of luggage memorializes Samson's great strength, and one of Gideon's jars adorns the cover of the Bible to be found in hotel rooms across the world.

Samson (Judges 13–16) was a huge man of great strength. He wrought havoc among the Philistines who ruled Israel during his time. He fell in love with Delilah, whom the Philistines paid to reveal the secret of his strength. After much cajoling, Samson confided to her that his long hair was a symbol of his devotion to God, and that if his head were shaved, his strength would vanish. While Samson slept, with Delilah's help, the Philistines cut his long hair. His strength left him. Thus did the Philistines shackle Samson, put out his eyes, and confine him to prison. They made the mistake, however, of bringing him out for public taunting at a community celebration, by which time Samson's hair had grown back, so that he pulled down the pillars of the building in which the celebration was being held, killing everyone.

The Book of Ruth provides a further tale from this era, a love story. During a famine in Israel, an Israelite woman named Naomi traveled with her husband and two sons into Moab seeking food. While there, both sons married Moabite women. Naomi's husband and both her sons soon died, however, leaving her with two daughters-in-law of foreign extraction. Deciding to return to Israel, Naomi bid both young women to return to their families in Moab,

AROUND THE WORLD

The period of the judges probably occurred in the 12th and 11th centuries B.C.E.

During this same time in India, the world's first known calendar, based on the lunar cycle, was developed.

In California, the Centennial Stump, a giant sequoia, began its growth around 1031 B.C.E. The tree lived until 1874 C.E.

In China, an imperial decree (1116 B.C.E.) stated that it was the requirement of the heavenly powers that the people regularly take a moderate amount of alcoholic drink.

where they would be provided for. One daughter-in-law did, but the other, Ruth, voiced a pledge of loyalty that has become well known: "Where you go, I will go; where you lodge, I will lodge; your people shall be my people, and your God my God" (Ruth 1:16). Returning to Israel with Naomi, Ruth went to glean the previously harvested fields of a rich man named Boaz, to gather bits of grain left by the harvesters. Boaz, returning from Bethlehem, saw the young woman in his field. One thing led to another, and Ruth became Boaz's wife, thus securing a home for Naomi. Ruth bore to Boaz a son, Obed, who became the father of Jesse, the father of the great King David. Thus did God use the faithfulness of a Moabite woman to redeem both the widow Naomi and, later, Israel itself.

From the ups and downs recounted in the Book of Judges we learn that local autonomy, as good as it sometimes sounds, was both blessing and curse in Israel. Not only did the nation have repeated trouble with military defense, but it also fell into terrible internal feuding (Judges 20–21), so that the author of Judges, at the end of the book, comments, "In those days there was no king in Israel; all the people did what was right in their own eyes" (Judges 21:25). This subtle remark hides great rancor. Anarchy is hardly a condition to be desired.

FOR DELIBERATION

1. The era of the judges was dominated by rural life: by farms and small villages. It would soon be followed by urbanization and centralization. There has been endless debate as to whether rural life represents pristine purity or backward traditionalism, and as to whether urban life is exciting and invigorating or frenzied and dehumanizing. What are some of the benefits and some of the drawbacks of country living? Of city living?

2. In the ancient world, it was almost unheard of for women to play significant roles in political or military events. And yet, Judges reports that God worked through Deborah and Jael to liberate Israel from the Canaanites. Can you name people God has used to accomplish big things, even though their society and culture es-

teemed them very little? What does this say about God? What
does it say about us?

3. Describe the picture of Naomi you get from reading the story of
   Ruth. Describe the picture of Ruth. Assuming that this story was
   not told simply as a moral lesson (i.e., "We should all be faithful as
   Ruth was"), what point do you think the author wanted to make?
   What is the author saying about God?

4. Gideon was a very fearful man, needing repeated proof from God
   that God would be with him in battle against the Midianites. And
   yet, Gideon courageously used terror, far more than military
   strength, to subdue Midian, using a mere 300 soldiers to smash
   clay jars and let out mighty war whoops to throw the camp of
   Midian into panic. Can you think of a time in your life when you
   had to set aside your own deep fears to act courageously? Some
   leaders appear to be absolutely fearless in their pursuits; do you
   think they are?

5. Samson was a man of great strength, but also of great vulnerability. Name one or two of your own strengths that you know, deep
   within you, are accompanied by vulnerability. Recount a story
   that illustrates the point.

6. John Calvin believed that the worst of all human social conditions is anarchy, where "all the people (do) what is right in their
   own eyes," and no rule regulates anyone. Calvin considered that
   any tyranny is better than anarchy. Would you agree or disagree?

10

The United Monarchy

The Book of 1 Samuel opens with the Philistines, Israel's neighbors to the southwest, menacing them once again, successfully routing the Israelite force and killing about four thousand men (1 Sam. 4). Wondering why God had abandoned them in this critical battle, Israel brought the ark of the covenant onto the battlefield, looking to install God in the midst of their fighting force. But God refused to be manipulated. The strategy failed miserably. Thirty thousand more Israelites were killed, and the Philistines captured the ark. Israel's heart sank. But the Philistines did not keep the ark for long: they were only too glad to return it when its presence in their towns led to outbreaks of disease and plagues. The ark was placed in the custody of a young Israelite priest, Eleazar, in the town of Kiriath-jearim.

In the midst of all this, God raised up a new judge, Samuel, who led Israel in battle and drove the Philistines from Israelite territory (1 Sam. 7:3-11).

These difficult events, however, led Israel to think new thoughts. Did they need a king? Was local autonomy insufficient for national security? Would judges continue to rise up in times of trouble? Could Israel survive forever without the central leadership that a monarch could provide? A lively debate followed (1 Sam. 8).

NUMBERS

Numbers in the Bible are often meant to be interpreted symbolically rather than literally.

The number *three* suggests "from heaven" or "heavenly," as in the early Christians coming to understand God as Father, Son, and Holy Spirit.

Four suggests "earthly" or "in earth," as in the four corners of the earth.

Five and *ten* suggest "a good, considerable number." Multiples of five and ten mean "a whole lot," and large multiples mean "a huge number." Thus, *thirty thousand* in this story of Israel's war with the Philistines probably refers not to an exact body count, but rather a very large number.

Six is the number of human beings, whom God made on the sixth day of creation. Because it is seven minus one, six also means "incomplete" or "unfinished." It is also used as a symbol of evil, as in the case of the Antichrist in the Book of Revelation, whose number is 666.

Seven suggests "complete," "finished," as in the seven days of creation.

Twelve depicts "God's people," "the church," as in the twelve tribes of Israel, or the twelve disciples of Jesus.

Forty suggests "a number of preparation," as in Israel's forty years in the wilderness or Jesus' forty days in the desert.

Numbers are especially symbolic in the Bible's apocalyptic writings — which include the Book of Daniel, the Revelation, and other smaller texts — but their symbolism often finds its way into the larger biblical story as well.

Those who favored monarchy contended that Israel needed a king to unify the nation, that a king would both govern the people and lead the nation in battle more effectively.

Those opposed to monarchy contended that a king would conscript Israel's young men into his army, draft their young women to work in his personal service, demand tax money to support him, and require choice fields to give to his favored friends, that he would return Israel to the same slavery from which God had delivered them in Egypt. They contended that God was the only king Israel needed, and that an earthly king would be an offense to the Almighty.

FREEDOM VERSUS DEFENSE

The debate in Israel was mostly over military security: was it more important to defend the nation or to maintain the people's freedom? Now that Israel had become an international presence, must a strong, dominant figure run — and possibly ruin — its life? Must self-determination (our modern term would be "civil liberties") be sacrificed for the sake of national defense? The question is both ancient and modern.

Israel was apparently more intent on securing itself. They wanted a king. There continued to be, through subsequent ages, a minority voice that did not believe this was God's wish. There were also liturgical celebrations that proclaimed God as king (Psalms 93–99 were some of the liturgies), events that must have made Israel's earthly kings less secure in their unbridled sense of power.

One of the enormous legacies ancient Israel gave to the world is the awareness that kings need to be criticized by countervailing voices. Far from possessing a direct communication pipeline with the Almighty, kings are subject to forms of blindness that keep them from seeing clearly. Power breeds an arrogance that seriously blurs vision. There need to be voices that speak other points of view, powers that balance the king's power. Kings need to be called to task, in the name of God, when they engage in haughty, self-serving behavior — which, because they are human beings, they will dependably do. And the right of dissent needs to be institutionalized, so thoroughly implanted in the nation's tradition that no king can depose it. As much as the king will disdain opposition voices, the debate needs to be viewed as loyal, not unpatriotic. In ancient Israel, the voices who spoke the different word from God were called prophets.

The first king in Israel was Saul. "There was not a man among the people of Israel more handsome than he; from his shoulders upward he was taller than any of the people" (1 Sam. 9:2). Saul successfully led

THE UNITED STATES GOVERNMENT

The United States government was founded with precisely these issues in mind. At the head of the government is a president, who holds some of the powers of a king — including the power to protect the nation militarily and to enforce the nation's laws internally. But the president is not fully to be trusted. The president is not empowered to make laws. Lawmaking is in the hands of a congress of representatives. And even this congress is divided into two bodies that must agree, so that neither has unbounded power. And as if this were not enough "check and balance," neither Congress nor the president is given the power to interpret the law. Law interpretation is vested in the Supreme Court.

This system embodied the best wisdom of the nation's founders on how, at one and the same time, to provide order and security, but also freedom. It is a precarious and delicate system, always in danger of being abused or subverted. Even in a check-and-balance system, leaders who wish to manipulate or exploit the people for their own ends can find ways to do it.

Israel in battle against the Amalekites and other neighboring king-doms. His entire reign involved him in battle against the Philistines. Despite moderate successes, however, Saul turned out to be a deeply unsettled and disturbed man, envious of those around him and prone to suspicion and bouts of depression. Deeply anxious before one military engagement, he consulted a medium, an act which Israelite law condemned in the strongest of terms. Saul was finally killed in battle (1 Sam. 31).

Israel's next king, however, would be hailed through all generations as its greatest. David was a preeminently successful military commander; eventually he would thoroughly defeat Israel's arch-enemy at the time, the Philistines, along with other armies that menaced the nation. He established his capital city at Jerusalem, at the summit of Mt. Zion, by overthrowing the Jebusites who lived there (2 Sam. 5:6-10). It was an ideal place for a capital city, easy to defend and liberally supplied with water from an underground spring (see p. 10). David brought the ark of God to Jerusalem and placed it in a special tent (2 Sam. 6). Hiram, king of the neighboring nation of Tyre, hearing of David's great success, sent carpenters and masons and cedar wood and built a house for the king (2 Sam. 5:11). Thus did Israel enjoy a time of peace, during which King David took many wives and fathered numerous children (2 Sam. 5:12-13).

God made a covenant with David through the prophet Nathan (2 Sam. 7), promising to establish "a place" for Israel and to "plant them" there, guaranteeing that evildoers and enemies would afflict them no more. God promised to establish David's descendants as the rulers in that place "forever." God warned that, if they sinned, chastisement would certainly follow. But God promised never to take away God's love from them. "Your house and your kingdom shall be made sure forever before me," said God, "your throne shall be established forever" (2 Sam. 7:16).

This Davidic covenant became the official faith of the nation of Israel (and later the southern kingdom of Judah) for the next four hundred years. God will maintain Jerusalem as an inviolable, safe place forever! God will sustain David and his descendants on Jerusalem's throne forever! God seals this promise by surrounding the city with steadfast love, which will never be removed. Israel spoke this theology in their poetry, sang it in their music, voiced it in their prophecies, and believed it to the depth of their being.

Here a word is in order about prophets in Israel. Prophets come and go throughout the biblical story without much explanation of who they are or where they come from. There seem to have been two kinds. First were the official royal advisors, prophets whose job it was to consult God concerning what the king proposed to do. These prophets were housed, fed, and paid by the king, so they most often made it their business to tell the king what he wanted to hear. Occasionally, however, one of them would break ranks, risk job and life, and report pointedly God's contrary word. Nathan was one of these prophets, and so was Isaiah many years later.

From somewhere — no one knows where, except that Israel's theology bred it — came a second group of independent prophets. These individuals simply appeared, in response to God's call, and proclaimed, often from the temple or palace steps, what God had to say about the king's policies. Their words were taken very seriously, often resulting in royal denunciation. Whether there was a fellowship of independent prophets, a line that ran from one generation to another, no one knows. What is known is that some of Israel's clearest, strongest, and most eloquent voices came from this independent set — Elijah, Amos, Micah, Jeremiah, and Ezekiel.

You and I usually think of a prophet as a person who accurately sees the future, one who specializes in prediction. In some measure, that was true in ancient Israel; prophets often reported visions of what was to come. But something else was more significant. A prophet was a person who accurately perceived *the present*, who looked at the current moment and assessed it correctly. Very often those in power do not, cannot, will not see accurately what is going on in their own domain. Few kings find advisors who will tell them the full truth. The independent prophets looked at present reality, described truthfully what they saw, and spoke God's word and heart about it. In return for this service, they were criticized, castigated, tortured, and sometimes killed. Representing the perspective of God before human power is most often a high-hazard occupation, even when that power sponsors royal prayer breakfasts and other public shows of personal faith. Prophecy has never been for the weak of heart.

For all his greatness, King David was hardly perfect, and nowhere is this more evident than in the story of Bathsheba. A beautiful woman, the wife of a soldier in David's army, Bathsheba was taking a bath one day in her house. David caught sight of her from his rooftop and desperately wanted to possess her. At his command, she came to his house. He committed adultery with her, and she became pregnant. This began a lengthy, sordid plot in which David tried to hide his guilt. The episode ended with the murder of Bathsheba's husband at David's command.

After all this, Nathan the prophet appeared before David and spoke God's severe judgment on David's sin. (Miraculously, Nathan's words did not cost him his life.) The child with whom Bathsheba was pregnant died soon after birth, causing David and his household severe suffering and grief. Nathan told David that because of his sin, although God was forgiving him, the king would never enjoy a peaceful family life.

The reign of King David saw high drama and some of the most vivid storytelling in the Bible. In one instance (2 Sam. 13–14), David's son, Amnon, became passionately infatuated with his beautiful sister, Tamar. With the advice of his friend Jonadab, Amnon devised a plot and raped his sister. When the rape was done, the storyteller says, "Amnon hated her with very great hatred; so that the hatred with which he hated her was greater than the love with which he had loved her" (2 Sam. 13:15, RSV). Another of David's sons, Absalom, killed Amnon in retribution. Absalom fled to exile in Geshur, lest his father kill him. After three years, a wise woman from the town of Tekoa ap-

CONFESSION

Psalm 51 is described in its superscript as "A psalm of David, when the prophet Nathan came to him, after he had gone in to Bathsheba."

"Have mercy on me, O God," the psalmist asks, "according to your steadfast love; according to your abundant mercy blot out my transgressions. Wash me thoroughly from my iniquity, and cleanse me from my sin."

This psalm, as well as the whole Bathsheba account, represents a remarkable phenomenon. Human beings, especially kings, rarely admit wrong. We will happily recite all the good things we have done and tout our greatness. But rarely do we confess our sin. In our modern day, as in the past, admitting wrong is considered weak, shameful.

The "prayer of confession" which we say in worship is the most counter-cultural activity in the church's life. In it, we say before God that we are a self-serving people who do wrong things, and we ask God for forgiveness and newness of life. It is very important that churches lead their parishioners in this activity. No other institution in the society does so. Can you imagine the Republican or Democratic Party opening a national convention with a prayer of confession? And yet, the only way to "create in me a clean heart," and to "put a new and right spirit within me" is with honesty about ourselves. Healing starts with confession.

We need the David/Bathsheba story in our history and Psalm 51 in our prayers.

peared before the king. "I am a widow," she said. "I had two sons. They quarreled in the field. The one struck the other and killed him. My family now demands, 'Give up the killer to avenge the life of his brother!' Thus would they quench the final ember in my life and leave me desolate." The king replied, "Your last son will be spared; I will give orders." To which the wise woman of Tekoa said, "Well, sir, if the king will spare my son, might it be that the king will also forgive his own son?" In the heart of this woman, who loved murdered and murderer because they were both her sons, do we see the heart of God.

As conflicted as his reign was, King David made Israel a successful and powerful nation. And he enjoyed a long rule, from 1000 to 961 B.C.E.

David was followed on the throne by his son, Solomon. If David was a successful military strategist, Solomon was a successful economic leader. He built the first Jerusalem temple, a splendid and magnificent place, God's home, where the ark of the covenant was set. He held an enormous assembly of all Israel for the dedication of the temple. Solomon set up trade with nations near and far, enriching the land as no one had ever imagined. He became known through generations for his wisdom and the glory of his wealth.

Solomon made one vast mistake, however. To carry out his massive building projects, he conscripted forced labor from his own people (1 Kings 5:13), turning fellow Israelites into slaves. The tactic bred deep hostility. When Solomon died, the ten northern tribes, from

WOODEN-HEADEDNESS

In 1984, Barbara Tuchman published a book entitled *The March of Folly*. In it she speaks of "wooden-headedness," the tendency of rulers not to be able to see, despite more than ample advice, how their own policies are undermining the success of their rule. Rulers often destroy themselves, Tuchman believed, because they cannot, or will not, see clearly what they are doing. One of Tuchman's case studies was King Solomon, the great ruler, famous for his wisdom, whose success was destroyed by his own slave labor policy — carried forward despite the advice of his best advisors.

whom the forced labor had come, seceded in protest and set up a separate kingdom (1 Kings 12:1-19). This ended the united monarchy and created two nations, Ephraim (or Israel) in the north and Judah (including the tribes of Judah and Benjamin) in the south. Solomon's prosperous, and in many ways successful, reign had stretched from 961 to 922 B.C.E.

A fundamental shift was taking place in Israel through this era of the united monarchy. Not only was local autonomy being replaced by kingship, but other forces of centralization were shaping the culture. The population moved from being almost exclusively rural to being significantly urban. Many people moved from farms to cities, causing urban areas to grow. Wealth began to be gained not only from agriculture but also from business. The ancient land-based economy was supplemented by a trade economy. Israel's military transformed. Formerly the army had been a volunteer band of patriots who rallied to oppose an invading foe and then disbanded until the next occasion. Now it became a standing force hired, trained, and paid by the king. And, while all this was happening, religion was changing drastically. In the period of the judges, religious ceremonies had been conducted by community priests at local shrines. Each little community or village had had its own worship site. Now, a central temple was constructed in Jerusalem and an order of priests established to preside. The religious devotion of common people might still involve local shrines, but now there was also a "big first church" (as it were) in the capital city. There would develop a competition between local priests and the temple priesthood for money and status. Neither would look with great charity upon the other.

All these happenings together meant that Israel was undergoing massive centralization: centralization of political rule, of population, of the economy, of military organization, and of religion. The difficulties of this change for a nation of former nomads and now farmers was huge.

Some people figured out quickly and profitably how to live in cities; others never did. Some made good merchants, others never developed business sense. Some learned to play the system, others fell through the cracks. Some grew sophisticated and successful, others failed.

As a result, an economic class division arose in Israel, a totally new phenomenon in the nation's life. While they were in the countryside, no one had been strikingly rich and no one severely poor. In the city, that changed. Successful Israelites dominated the political, economic, and religious arenas, while many at the bottom were poor and powerless. This occurrence in Abraham's family, among the people God had delivered from Egypt and given the rich land flowing with milk and honey, became a rank contradiction for the faith. It made the rich and powerful very happy, but it made God exceedingly unhappy. Wealth disparity became a recurring theme through the years that followed, as we will see.

RICH AND POOR IN ANCIENT ISRAEL

Roland de Vaux writes tellingly of the archaeological evidence for wealth disparity in ancient Israel: "At Tirsah, the modern Tell el-Farah near Nablus, the houses of the tenth century B.C. are all of the same size and arrangement. Each represents the dwelling of a family which lived in the same way as its neighbors. The contrast is striking when we pass to the eighth century houses on the same site: the rich houses are bigger and better built and in a different quarter from the poorer houses which are huddled together.

"Between these two centuries, a social revolution had taken place." (*Ancient Israel*, pp. 72-73)

FOR DELIBERATION

1. How much freedom do you think we should we give up to maintain security? How much insecurity should we risk to maintain freedom? There has long been profound disagreement over these

questions. On a one-to-ten scale, where "total freedom" is one and "maximum security" is ten, locate yourself. Why do you feel the way you do?

2. The first amendment to the U.S. Constitution tries to guarantee that voices of dissent in our country shall not be silenced. Many other nations have laws to this effect as well. Why do you think America's founders believed this so important as to make it the *first* amendment? If both the national leader and most of the people feel that particular newspapers or news commentators are wrong, can those be justifiably silenced?

3. Describe someone you know of who seems to have particular talent for reading accurately the present moment, for analyzing correctly things or events that are nearby.

4. Can you name someone in our lifetime who has been effective at speaking hard and difficult words to our nation's leadership, at playing Nathan's role? What made that person effective?

5. Has there been a time when your admission of your guilt has accomplished what Psalm 51 says in verses 10-12?

6. Where have you experienced Barbara Tuchman's "woodenheadedness" in yourself? When have you been blind to things going on right beneath your eyes?

7. Why, in two hundred years, would an egalitarian nation of equally shared resources turn into a hierarchical nation of pronounced wealth disparity? Would it happen primarily because of a lack of initiative and skill among those who became poor? Would it happen primarily because of a lack of morals and human sensitivity among those who became rich?

11

The Beginning of the Divided Monarchy

The two nations went their separate ways, still blood kin but now distinctly apart. The kingdom of Israel in the north, sometimes called Ephraim, consisted of ten tribes and was led by King Jeroboam. The kingdom of Judah in the south, consisting of the two tribes of Judah and Benjamin, was led by King Rehoboam, Solomon's son. Israel's capital city, after a brief period, became Samaria. Judah's capital remained Jerusalem.

A main difference between the two nations was in the way each selected its kings. In Judah, the successor of a king was to be the king's son. Reflecting God's covenant promise to David, Judah believed that their royal succession was to maintain the Davidic line. This created a well-defined procedure and stable transitions.

In Israel, it was believed that when a king died, God would designate afresh the successor. Some person who showed special aptitude or strength, some person whose birth had been associated with unusual natural signs, would rise up to rule. This created far less stability, with would-be successors competing for the job. Assassinations were not infrequent.

In this and the following two chapters, we will touch only on the highlights of this long, often troubled time in the history of God's people.

The many interactions between King Ahab of Israel and the prophet Elijah are some of the best known from this period. In 874 B.C.E., Ahab became king in Israel. Ahab worshiped foreign gods and, as part of his international treaty-making, took as his wife Jezebel, daughter of the king of Sidon in Lebanon. Jezebel was a devoted worshiper of the fertility god Baal, and Ahab built an altar to Baal in Samaria. He also built a sacred pole, a phallic symbol used in Baal worship.

God called Elijah, a man from the town of Tishbe, to speak against Ahab. At God's bidding, Elijah declared to Ahab, "As the Lord God of Israel lives, before whom I stand, there shall be neither dew nor rain these years, except by my word" (1 Kings 17:1). An enormous drought descended upon Israel, a dry season that would end only when Ahab returned the nation to faithfulness.

Having announced the drought, Elijah went into hiding (1 Kings 17:8-16). At first he camped in the wilderness by one of the seasonal wadis (see Chapter 2); but when it dried up he lived with a widow in Zarephath of Lebanon. The widow had a jar of meal and a jug of oil from which she, her son, and Elijah ate and drank. God promised that neither jar nor jug would become empty until God sent rain upon Israel.

After three years of drought, in which Israel suffered mightily, all the while imploring Baal to send rain, God told Elijah to present himself before Ahab (1 Kings 18). Ahab, at Elijah's bidding, assembled all Israel at Mt. Carmel west of Jezreel. He gathered there also the four hundred prophets of Baal who were employed in the royal court. Elijah and the prophets of Baal then had a contest, to see who could bring down fire from heaven to consume the animal sacrifice each had prepared. The court prophets begged half the day that Baal would consume their sacrifice, but nothing happened. Elijah's sacrifice, on the other hand, was instantaneously consumed. The Israelites seized the Baal prophets and killed them. And soon after, rain descended upon Israel, ending the drought. This event enshrined Elijah in Israel's memory for millennia — as a prophet who, at great personal sacrifice, obeyed the voice of God and was vindicated. It by no means, however, ended Israel's infatuation with fertility-god worship. Cultic prostitution held a lasting allure.

Nor did it bring Ahab to faithfulness. An Israelite named Naboth owned a vineyard in the fertile Valley of Jezreel (1 Kings 21). King Ahab, who lived in a house nearby, admired Naboth's vineyard and wanted it for a vegetable garden. He offered to buy it from Naboth or to swap some other piece of land for it. Naboth refused, stating that the land was his family's inheritance and that to sell it would transgress God's gift. Jezebel, Ahab's foreign wife who had no regard for Israelite religion, seized the vineyard and had Naboth murdered by thugs. She presented the land as a gift to her husband. At God's bidding, the prophet Elijah declared to Ahab that in the same place where dogs had licked up Naboth's blood, dogs would lick up his blood. God, through a prophet named Micaiah, lured Ahab into a disastrous battle against the kingdom of Aram, and Elijah's prophecy came to pass.

A prophet who succeeded Elijah, Elisha, performed memorable signs and wonders in Israel in the years that followed (2 Kings 1–13), conveying God's will to the often wayward nation.

AROUND THE WORLD

In 814 B.C.E., Carthage, on the north coast of Africa, was founded by Phoenician traders. Carthage would become one of the greatest cities of the ancient Mediterranean world.

Between 800 and 750 B.C.E., Homer was writing the *Iliad* and the *Odyssey*.

In 776 B.C.E., the Olympic games were born in Greece.

In 753 B.C.E., legend has it that the city of Rome was founded by Romulus as a refuge for runaway slaves and murderers.

FOR DELIBERATION

1. Would you prefer to live in a kingdom where the king was automatically the eldest son of the previous king, or in a nation where each new king was chosen "by the spirit"? What would be the assets and liabilities in each way?

2. God was clearly with Elijah, working great acts of divine power through him. And yet, Elijah seems to have lived a tortured mental life, battling his own emotions and confidence all along the way. As a person close to God, why didn't Elijah "have it easy" emotionally? Why did he have to wrestle so much with self-doubt? Can you think of others in the Bible who had the same problem?

3. Elijah stands as a giant figure in Jewish tradition. At the *seder*, the Jewish celebration of Passover, a room door is left open, Elijah's door, so that the ancient prophet can enter to be with those celebrating. What message does Elijah's encounter with God and with the prophets of Baal speak to you?

12

Great Struggle and Great Hope

Many years and many kings after Ahab, Israel enjoyed one of the most prosperous periods in its history under King Jeroboam II (786-746 B.C.E.). Business boomed, due in large measure to international trade across the region. Those who were successful lived in fine houses, bathing themselves in expensive oils, dining on rich food, devising for themselves pleasing songs on stringed musical instruments, sleeping in ornately styled beds. People who could afford it possessed summer homes and winter homes. The social elites held extravagant parties where the wine and other strong drink flowed

TWO KINDS OF REVOLUTION

The early American economist John Taylor wrote these words about revolution: "There are two modes of invading private property: the first, by which the poor plunder the rich, is sudden and violent: the second, by which the rich plunder the poor, [is] slow and legal." (*An Inquiry into the Principles and Policy of the Government of the United States*, 1814) freely. The sanctuaries of worship were full of believers who were certain that their prosperity meant that God's face was smiling on them. Offerings flowed abundantly. It was the best of times for the well-off.

But it was the worst of times for many thousands of other Israelites. A sizable percentage of the population lived not in fine homes but in huts and hovels. They did not eat lambs from the herd or calves from the midst of the stall, but whatever bits and morsels they could scavenge. They were easy prey in the marketplace, victims of unscrupulous merchants who cheated them routinely. They were even easier prey in Israel's courts, where judicial decisions were bought and sold. Some among the prosperous competed to see who could cheat the poor most cunningly.

Thus did Israel have its first flirtation with a belief that became highly popular among the well-off of many different times and places: the belief that because they were economically successful, they were also morally good; and because they were both economically successful and morally good, they deserved to rule the community. The prosperous were convinced that it was they who were best suited for making and administering the nation's laws, they to whom God had given superior wisdom for leading the rest. This belief in divine favor toward the successful glued in place a wealth disparity that tortured Israel for the rest of its life as a nation.

Into this setting of vast ill-distribution of wealth and power stepped Amos, the first of Israel's prophets whose sayings have been collected and preserved in a book bearing his name. Amos, though a native of a village called Tekoa in Judah, prophesied in Samaria, in the northern kingdom of Israel, sometime around 750 B.C.E. He probably spoke his words from the steps of the religious sanctuary or the king's palace. Amos declared that, just as God had paralyzed with fear the armies that opposed Israel when God gave them the Promised Land, God was now going to paralyze with fear the army of Israel as another nation, Assyria, removed them from that land (Amos 2:12-16). Amos proclaimed harsh judgment for Israel's gross perversion of God's intent for the land. Amos pointed to the economic swindling that was daily fare in the marketplace (Amos 2:6-7; 4:1; 5:11); to injustice in the legal system, which was easy for those of money to buy (Amos 5:10); to a general disregard by the powerful and prosperous for their poor brothers and sisters (Amos 6:4-6).

Disdaining Israel's public show of piety (Amos 4:4-5), Amos deliv-

WEALTH DISPARITY

In 1889, Andrew Carnegie, who had amassed an enormous fortune by producing iron and steel for America's railways, wrote an essay on wealth disparity. Entitled "Wealth," the essay set forth the reasons why Carnegie was convinced that immense wealth concentrated in the hands of a few individuals served the highest common good. "The man of wealth," Carnegie wrote, ". . . [is] strictly bound as a matter of duty to administer in the manner which, in his judgment, is best calculated to produce the most beneficial result for the community — the man of wealth thus becoming the sole agent and trustee for his poorer brethren, bringing to their service his superior wisdom, experience, and ability to administer — doing for them better than they would or could do for themselves." Carnegie believed that "the laws upon which civilization was founded" naturally amassed wealth into the hands of a few bright, able, exceptionally gifted people, and that those people were obligated to expend their excess wealth lifting the common masses. Carnegie called this the "gospel of wealth." His personal strategy for carrying it out included funding the construction of public libraries all across the country. Carnegie's public libraries have made a significant contribution to the nation's education. But for all his good intentions, he seemed blind to the ways in which his steel factories exploited, bullied, and demeaned the labor that manufactured his wealth, not to mention the arrogance inherent in assuming that he possessed superior wisdom for knowing what was best for poor people.

> ## THE FIFTIES
>
> In a book called *The Fifties,* journalist David Halberstam contends that the United States of the 1950s was by no means the first rich nation in the history of the world, that there had been other rich nations before, but the United States was the first rich nation in the history of the world in which its wealth was distributed across great masses of the population, enabling common people to purchase Mr. Ford's automobiles and Mr. Levitt's mass-produced suburban homes, and to feel that they possessed a genuine stake in America's prosperity. Halberstam considers this broad wealth distribution to be one of 1950s America's greatest strengths.

ered God's word: "I hate, I despise your [religious] festivals, and I take no delight in your solemn assemblies, . . . but let justice roll down like waters, and righteousness like an everflowing stream" (Amos 5:21, 24), words later prophets of God would appropriate. Amos's primary prophetic attack was on Israel's religious certainties, its confidence that God was solidly on its side in maintaining things as they were. These prophetic attacks occur all through the book (i.e., Amos 5:18-20, where Amos turns "the day of the Lord" from the popularly anticipated day of great national victory into a day of bitter and crushing defeat). Amos believed that God would be faithful to the covenant promises, redeeming Israel as a servant nation of God's will (Amos 9:11-15), but that it would happen only after the punishment and exile (Amos 9:1-4). Amos, as faithful as he was to God's call, is not a person most of us would want as our next-door neighbor.

Momentous change was happening all across the ancient Near East during this time. David, Solomon, and their immediate successors had been able to make Israel appear strong and mighty only because of a quirk in the region's history. Since the latter-middle part of the third millennium B.C.E., the truly strong kingdoms of the ancient

JUDGMENT AND PROMISE

The first eight and a half chapters of Amos are filled with God's judgment. The final half chapter speaks God's promise. This sets a pattern followed by other Old Testament prophets. The God who will punish will also redeem. The points to be drawn from this pattern seem to be several.

- God never punishes without a greater redemptive purpose. Punishment by itself is never God's way.
- Punishment is part of the God-human relationship, just as blessing is. Punishment does not ever mean that God has severed the relationship, though it may seem that way to us.
- The promises of God are stronger than any evil we human beings can do. We cannot cause God to cancel what God has vowed.
- God's absolute bottom line is a loving heart. Yes, there can be disappointment, there can be anger, there can be fury — our evil is never taken lightly. But after all else has happened, it is compassion that will prevail in God.

Near East had all been in decline. Egypt, Babylon, and Assyria had been suffering internal problems and were weakened. It was only in such a power vacuum that tiny Israel could step forward and think of itself as formidable.

In the mid-eighth century, however, Assyria began to pull itself together. Capable Assyrian leaders emerged. Any observer with eyes to see, like Amos, discerned quickly that the future would not be like the past. Amos prophesied that God would use Assyria to execute God's fierce judgment against an Israel that had badly misused God's gift.

In 742 B.C.E., in the time of Amos, God also called a prophet in the south, in Judah, named Isaiah. Isaiah was a very young man, working in the Jerusalem temple. While there one day, Isaiah encountered the awesome, overwhelming Presence of God and was called to speak to the nation the words God placed in his mouth (Isa. 6).

"The ox knows its owner, the ass knows its master's crib," Isaiah began, "but Israel does not know, my people do not understand" (Isa. 1:3). The dumb animals have a keener perception than God's people do!

Like Amos in the north, Isaiah chided the wealthy and powerful for amassing unto themselves so many houses, so many fields, that there was no place left for anyone else to live (Isa. 5:8). He likened the nation to a vineyard, planted by God, from which God expected sweet grapes. But the vineyard yielded wild grapes, grapes that set the teeth on edge with their sourness (Isa. 5). He declared woe upon "those who drag iniquity along with cords of falsehood" (Isa. 5:18), "who call evil good and good evil" (Isa. 5:20). "How the faithful city [Jerusalem] has become a whore!" Isaiah proclaimed. "She that was full of justice — [with] righteousness lodged in her — but now murderers!" (Isa. 1:21) "Your princes are rebels and companions of thieves. Everyone loves a bribe and runs after gifts. They do not defend the orphan, and the widow's cause does not come before them" (Isa. 1:23).

Meanwhile Isaiah's contemporary, the prophet Micah, excoriated his people's devotion to religious ritual while powerless brothers and sisters around them languished in neglect. "With what shall I come before the Lord, and bow myself before God on high? Shall I come before him with burnt offerings, with calves a year old? Will the Lord be pleased with thousands of rams, with ten thousands of rivers of oil? Shall I give my firstborn for my transgression, the fruit of my body for the sin of my soul? God has told you, O mortal, what is good; and what does the Lord require of you but to do justice, and to love mercy, and to walk humbly with your God" (Micah 6:6-8).

Tiglath-pileser III, the exceedingly vigorous and able king of Assyria, based in Haran on the Tigris River, brought his army into Palestine beginning around 745 B.C.E. By 738, he had exacted tribute from most of the small states in Syria and northern Palestine, including Israel.

After Assyria withdrew its army to fight battles on other fronts, a number of kings, Syria, Israel, the Philistines among them, formed a coalition to oppose the next incursion of the mighty giant. When ambassadors were sent to Jerusalem to recruit Judah's participation, Judah refused. Not willing to have a potentially hostile power in the midst of their coalition, the leaders invaded Judah (2 Kings 16:5), looking to depose Judah's King Ahaz and place a leader of their own choosing on the throne. Ahaz, facing impossible military odds, was addressed by his prophet Isaiah (Isa. 7). Stand firmly! Isaiah exhorted. God will protect Jerusalem, as God promised in the covenant made with King David! No military force will overthrow this holy place! Even the strongest coalition is no match for God!

In his prophecy, Isaiah declared that "the young woman," probably his wife, was pregnant and that the child she would bear would be named Immanuel, which means in Hebrew "God is with us." Before he grew even to the earliest stages of human discernment, Isaiah declared, the endangering coalition would disintegrate!

What King Ahaz did, apparently, was send tribute to Tiglath-pileser, begging him to come quickly and smash the opponents, a request with which Tiglath-pileser willingly complied! In 734 B.C.E., he marched on the coalition and utterly destroyed it. A year later, he was back, seizing land all across Galilee and Transjordan and deporting large portions of the population into exile.

Within a few years, Tiglath-pileser was succeeded by his son, Shalmaneser V. Israel's king, Hoshea, thinking this might be the time to rebel, withheld tribute. It was a disastrous calculation. Shalmaneser attacked Israel in 724. The capital city of Samaria held out for two years. But, with Sargon II having taken over in Assyria after the death of Shalmaneser, Samaria fell to the Assyrians in 721 B.C.E. The city was destroyed. According to Sargon, 27,290 citizens were deported into exile in various places across the Assyrian Empire, ultimately to lose their ethnic identity. The northern kingdom, Israel, would never recover. It was gone forever.

Judah, however, survived. Through the reign of King Ahaz (735-715 B.C.E.), Judah remained submissive to Assyria, paying heavy tribute. His son and successor, Hezekiah, however, reversed his father's policy. Hezekiah instituted a thoroughgoing religious reform, expelling Assyrian and all other foreign gods from Judah's worship. He refused to send tribute to Assyria and prepared to defend his independence.

Thus did Sargon's successor, Sennacherib, come to do battle with Judah and Jerusalem. Surrounding the city with his army, Sennacherib prepared to attack. All Jerusalem, including its king, trembled in fear. The prophet Isaiah, however, proclaimed to Hezekiah the same message he had proclaimed to Ahaz decades earlier, that God had promised to keep Jerusalem safe forever and that God would defend it now against the haughty pretensions of Assyria (Isa. 36–37). Isaiah declared that the Assyrians would not even shoot an arrow into the city or cast up a siege mound against it. What happened was startling! Here is what the Bible says: "The angel of the Lord set out and struck down one hundred eighty-five thousand in the camp of the Assyrians; when morning dawned, they were all dead bodies. Then King Sennacherib of Assyria left, went home, and lived in Nineveh" (Isa. 37:36-37). Assyria withdrew, leaving Jerusalem untouched!

Sennacherib returned with his powerful army in 701 B.C.E., quashing rebellions up and down the Mediterranean coast and waging enormous destruction in city after city, and spared Jerusalem only when Hezekiah sent him huge tribute and submitted Judah thoroughly to Assyrian vassalage.

This moment signaled the end of Judah's autonomy. Since Joshua had first conquered the Promised Land more than five hundred years earlier, the Israelites had largely enjoyed self-rule. The Near East power vacuum had provided the opportunity. With the rise of Assyria, however, everything changed. From 701 forward, the people of God would be ruled almost continuously by enormous foreign powers. The glory days of David and Solomon, when Israel paid tribute to no one and had no outside soldiers stationed on their soil, were gone. Life for God's people would be continued subjugation, a reality they would never willingly accept.

A further word is due about prophets of this era. The period from about 740 to 700 B.C.E. constituted one of the most violent and destructive times in Israel's history. Time and again, the Assyrians struck with brutal force. They destroyed cities, devastated fields, looted treasures, and killed or deported populations, expressing repeatedly their disdain for all things foreign. Assyria believed that they themselves were the greatest nation history had produced, the preeminent culture ever to appear on the human stage, and their rampages through Palestine left clear testimony to this arrogance. Israel bent low beneath the onslaught.

Out of this nearly half-century of destruction, what one modern scholar called "the first holocaust of the Jews," came a remarkable prophetic phenomenon. The prophets, though fully immersed in the turmoil, saw visions of peace nearly unparalleled in human history. Their people and land destroyed, they nevertheless maintained clear confidence that *this* was *not* what God destined for the creation, that God in a time to come would redeem humanity from its violent heart and bring *shalom*.

Isaiah (Isa. 2:1-4) and Micah (Mic. 4:1-4) spoke of the day when all the nations would see the glory of God and gather to learn God's ways. "They shall beat their swords into plowshares, and their spears into pruning hooks; nation shall not lift up sword against nation, neither shall they learn war any more."

Isaiah (Isa. 11:6-9) looked toward a day when "the wolf shall live with the lamb, and the leopard shall lie down with the kid, the calf and the lion and the fatling together, and a little child shall lead them," a vision of "the peaceable kingdom" rendered by numerous artists over the years.

In one moving passage, the prophet Hosea depicted God as a parent (Hosea 11), loving the nation of Israel as a child, teaching them to walk, leading them by the hand, feeding them with tender kindness — until Israel rebelled, refusing God's love, waging violence in their cities, plotting iniquity in their lives. God, in despair, vowed at first to send them back to Egypt, to release them to their own devices, to cut the covenant bonds. But then God, in deep contemplation, declared, No, I cannot do it! "How can I hand you over [to servitude]? My heart recoils within me. I will not execute my fierce anger, for I am God and no mortal, the Holy One in your midst." Hosea's scene gave an intimate view of God's emotional conflict over the stubbornness of this people. But it ended with a conclusion based on the character of God, not on human faithlessness.

Isaiah painted perhaps the most striking picture (Isa. 19:23-25). Isaiah saw the time coming when God would build a highway bridging the mighty superpowers, Assyria and Egypt, a highway on which Egyptians would freely travel into Assyria and Assyrians into Egypt, to worship the Lord together. On that day, Isaiah said, Israel would become "the third with Egypt and Assyria, whom the Lord of Hosts has blessed, saying, 'Blessed be Egypt my people, and Assyria the work of my hands, and Israel my heritage.'" To Isaiah's original audience, this vision would have been totally outlandish! Anyone who believed that the hearts of haughty Egypt and brutal Assyria would turn to humility had to be a fool! Either that, or a person of profound religious faith.

Through the hottest fires of international violence, Israel's prophets believed that God had promised peace, "very good," to the fallen creation, and that God's promise, not humanity's violence, would form the future. The worst blows history could inflict did not shake their conviction. The faith of these prophets was one of Israel's great gifts to the world.

For Deliberation

1. What current realities do you believe prophetic voices are calling us to see that most of us don't see? I, for instance, suspect that

there is emerging in America a subculture of relationally deprived children, children who have spent much time relating to TV sets and computers and little time relating to adult humans (especially parents), and that we have no idea what they will mean in our future. The prophetic voice that called my attention to this was my retired-schoolteacher neighbor who said, "There are too many children in today's world who don't have anyone they can disappoint."

2. Why is it that, in every society, the poor become easily invisible to the well-off? How is it that the two groups can live so close to one another and yet the rich cannot see the poor? What happens to our vision to cause that?

3. Do you believe, as many have, that one function of government should be to distribute a minimum level of wealth across the population? Or do you believe that market forces should be left totally free of government control? Or do you believe in something in between?

4. Look again at the sidebar entitled "Judgment and Promise" on page 83. Which of the "points to be drawn" seem most persuasive to you?

5. What do you think caused Isaiah, out of the bloodiest half-century in ancient Israel's life, to see magnificent visions of God's promised *shalom*? Where does such hope come from in the midst of raging despair?

6. Describe a situation in which the prophecy in Micah 4:1-4 has had special power and meaning for you. To whom do you think this message is most pointedly spoken in our time?

13

Reform, Destruction, and Exile

Assyria ruled Palestine, including the tiny nation of Judah, through most of the seventh century B.C.E. All the while, however, disintegration was setting in. Finally, in 612, a coalition of Medes and Babylonians ransacked the great Assyrian city of Nineveh and put Assyria to rout. By 610, the coalition had proceeded up the Euphrates River and had destroyed Haran in the north. A small remnant of the Assyrian army tried to retake Haran in 609 and was utterly destroyed. Assyria was finished.

King Josiah reigned in Judah from 640 to 609. With Assyrian domination weakening, Josiah engaged Judah in the most thoroughgoing religious reform in the nation's history (2 Kings 22:3–23:25). In 622, during repairs on the Jerusalem temple, an apparently old copy of "the book of the law" was found. Brought to the king's attention, it provoked in him profound concern. Josiah summoned the temple elders, read the book to them, and entered with them into a solemn covenant before God to lead the nation in obeying it. Foreign cults and practices were purged from Judah, including those from Assyrian religion. All personnel of foreign cults, including eunuch priests and prostitutes of both sexes, were put to death. Divination and magic were suppressed. The traditional religious shrine of the old northern kingdom at Bethel was destroyed and the priests there put to death. Josiah shut down outlying religious shrines throughout Judah, centralizing public worship in Jerusalem, and inviting rural priests to take their place among the temple clergy.

Probably the "book of the law" that inspired these measures was some form of our current Book of Deuteronomy. Actions taken correlate well with portions of that book.

Two prophets of this time, Zephaniah and the young Jeremiah, spoke messages entirely consonant with the reform. Judah was living under God's judgment, they declared, because of the idolatry and corruption commonly practiced across the nation. The time was short for repentance, and the retribution would be swift if there was none.

The immediate effect of Josiah's reform on the nation is difficult to evaluate; little evidence is available. The reform did, however, begin one trend that would become critically significant. Josiah's action began the process of implanting a written book of law at the center of Judah's life and theology. Before this time, the nation's relation to God had been understood through God's covenant with David, the promises God had made concerning Jerusalem and David's ancestors. Now, the nation's relationship with God hinged increasingly on obedience to the written legal code. Obey and live; disobey

---

AROUND THE WORLD

Around 640 B.C.E., humanity's first known coins were minted in Lydia (Turkey), featuring face-to-face heads of a bull and a lion.

In 624, invading Arabs established a military settlement in northern Egypt that would later be called Cairo.

Legend has it that around 600 B.C.E., Aesop, a former Phrygian slave and author of the famous collection of fables, said, "We hang the petty thieves, but appoint the great ones to public office."

and die (Deut. 30:15-20): this principle was becoming the center of Hebrew piety.

In 598 B.C.E., the army of Babylon, led by King Nebuchadnezzar, having inflicted heavy losses against the Egyptians, marched on Jerusalem. Judah, knowing they stood no chance in a conflict, surrendered. Eighteen-year-old King Jehoiachin, along with the queen mother, other high officials, and leading citizens, were taken to Babylon. A man named Zedekiah, a member of the king's family, was installed as ruler.

This setback seems only to have intensified fervor for rebellion, however. Continued agitation and sedition brought Nebuchadnezzar back in 588.

It was in this time that the prophet Jeremiah spoke most forcefully. Declaring that Judah's disobedience and idolatry had pushed God's patience beyond the limit, he discounted the promises of the Davidic covenant: "Why do you trust in these deceptive words, 'This is the temple of the Lord, the temple of the Lord, the temple of the Lord'" (Jer. 7:4). He admonished Judah to follow the exhortations of the law: "If you truly amend your ways and your doings, if you truly act justly one with another, if you do not oppress the alien, the orphan and the widow, or shed innocent blood in this place, and if you do not go after other gods to your own hurt, then I will dwell with you in this place, in the land I gave of old to your ancestors forever and ever . . . [but] will you steal, murder, commit adultery, swear falsely, make offerings to Baal, and go after other gods that you have not known, and then come and stand before me in this house, which is called by my name, and say, 'We are safe!' — only to go on doing all these abominations?" (Jer. 7:5-7, 9-10). Jeremiah warned endlessly of the need for national repentance, of the impending judgment, but his words fell mostly on unhearing ears.

In 587 B.C.E., the Babylonians penetrated Jerusalem's wall and poured in (2 Kings 25). The destruction was fierce. Nebuchadnezzar burned the city and leveled its walls. A large portion of its civil, military, and ecclesiastical leadership was put to death. The brightest and most able of those remaining were deported to refugee camps in Babylon. Various others fled to Egypt or other locations. The few who remained in Palestine tended to be a forlorn, bedraggled lot. The holy city lay in ruins, along with the theology that had guaranteed its well-being. The kingdom of Judah was dead forever.

A prophet named Ezekiel interpreted this event. Ezekiel saw a vision of a multi-wheeled vehicle, attended by living figures, that descended from the heavens upon Jerusalem (Ezek. 1). Because of the wickedness and idolatry of the city, the glory of God arose out of the holy temple, mounted the vehicle, and traveled off to a distant place. With this departure of the divine presence, faithless hordes overran the city and destroyed it.

This was a moment of critical trauma in the history of God's people. God had traveled with them out of Egypt, through the Sinai wilderness, into the Promised Land, and through four hundred years of national history. The glory of the Lord had dwelt among them through struggle, through danger, through contention, through war, through prosperity, through national celebration, and all in between — a continual presence. But now, God had abandoned them, left them to live by their own stubborn self-will at fate's mercy. The accompanying presence of the nation's God was gone, Ezekiel declared.

PRESENCE

After nearly four decades as a pastor, I am convinced that the most basic anxiety in the human heart concerns our need for "presence." Do I walk the paths of earth essentially alone, or does another accompany me? Am I by myself or not? The greatest curse in life is desolation: when there is no one who sees, no one who listens, no one who empathizes or cares. Desolation can happen anywhere: at home, at work, in a hospital, in a nursing home, in a crowded place. "Walking with" another human being, paying attention, knowing, caring, embodying the communion of spirits is the greatest gift we can give.

RESURRECTION

Can we rise from the dead? This question occurs throughout life. Can a nation destroyed and exiled, its property in ruins, its heart and soul defeated, rise up and discover new life? Can a slave people in Egypt, exploited, devalued, disregarded, become a strong kingdom? Can a fifty-year-old man who, for twenty-three years, has turned to alcohol to keep his mind off his failures and to settle his frustrations, escape the tyranny of addiction that has enslaved him? Can a halting family of refugees, escaping violence in their homeland, entering a new culture, a new language, a new style of life — can these find a future that is good? Can a mid-life married couple, children mostly grown, interests different, viewpoints diverging, bodies thickening, lives drifting apart — can these recover love for each other? Can a ninety-two-year-old woman confined to a nursing home, dependent on others for virtually everything, kindle a spark and light up her surroundings? Can one from whom life has departed find the prison gates of death thrown open and God's new creation presented as a gift? Can an earth whose air has been poisoned, whose rivers have been contaminated, whose wetlands have been drained and paved, whose mountains have been stripped, whose radio airwaves are filled with hatred, vitriol, and deception, whose spirit has turned to divisiveness and anger — can that earth somehow find a new way to live?

It is easy to believe that God was the Creator. It is much more challenging to believe that God can be the Re-creator.

The question occurs throughout human life: can we rise from the dead? Our human reaction, with Ezekiel, is strong skepticism, "Can that be, Lord?" In response, the Bible shouts an exclamatory, "Yes!"

But Ezekiel also saw another vision, too — of bones scattered across a valley (Ezek. 37:1-10), the bones of a people once alive but now slain. The bones were very dry; all the life had departed from them. "Can these bones live?" God's spirit said to Ezekiel. Ezekiel believed absolutely not, that dead bones do not come to life. But, at the spirit's urging, Ezekiel spoke to the bones (here we recognize echoes of the creative power of God's word in Genesis 1). Ezekiel told the bones to arise. There was a great rattling! The bones lived and fitted themselves together, "a vast multitude" (Ezek. 37:10)! (From this story, of course, came a well-known campfire song.)

Ezekiel's vision continued. When Jerusalem had been chastened, cleansed, and rebuilt, the glory of God returned on the same vehicle on which it had departed (Ezek. 43), to dwell in the midst of God's people once more. Ezekiel himself would not live long enough to see this restoration, but it was an integral part of his prophetic interpretation of the harsh, awful events of his time.

FOR DELIBERATION

1. How would Israel's religion have changed in the transition from a faith focused on promise to a faith focused on law? What are the pros and cons of promise-based faith; of a law-based faith? Which reflects more fully the faith you hold?

2. Describe a time when God seemed to have abandoned you, when everything went bad and your most fervent prayers brought no apparent answer. What went on inside you? Compare this with the psalmist's lament in Psalm 136. Have you ever "had it out with God" the way this psalmist did?

3. Even through the worst of tribulation, some people seem to bear a sturdy faith: "The Lord is with me!" Can you describe someone you have known with a faith like that? Does such a faith happen in you, or do you quickly crumble before adversity?

4. Tell of someone you know of who has, at least figuratively, risen from the dead.

14

Return

In 539 B.C.E., King Cyrus of Persia defeated Babylon. A year later, Cyrus decreed that the exiles of Israel were to return home to reestablish their country, their national identity, their religion, their life. Where Babylon had implemented a brutal policy of death or deportation to conquered peoples, Persia took a completely different approach. Cyrus honored the traditions of other nations and wished them to prosper, under his vassalage, of course, but still in relative autonomy. For its time, his was a remarkably enlightened and respectful foreign policy.

Another prophet arose in this moment to speak powerfully to Israel. We have no knowledge of this prophet's name; his oracles have been placed in the book of Isaiah, forming the final twenty-seven chapters of that book (40–66). This prophet is commonly called Second Isaiah. Declaring that the God of Israel was speaking through Cyrus's edict, Second Isaiah proclaimed, "Comfort, O comfort my people, says your God. Speak tenderly to Jerusalem, and cry to her that she has served her term, that her penalty is paid, that she has received from the Lord's hand double for all her sins" (Isa. 40:1-2). The prophet said that God was preparing a coronation procession from their exile camp, back across the desert to Jerusalem, a procession in which every valley would be lifted up and every mountain and hill made low, a regal parade that would crown God as king.

Addressing God's abandonment, Second Isaiah asked, "Why do you say, O Jacob, and speak, O Israel, 'My way is hidden from the Lord, and my right is disregarded by my God'?" (Isa. 40:27). "Those who wait for the Lord shall renew their strength, they shall mount up with wings like eagles, they shall run and not be weary, they shall walk and not faint" (Isa. 40:31).

Second Isaiah personified the restored Israel as God's servant, called not simply "to raise up the tribes of Jacob and to restore the survivors of Israel," but to serve as God's "light to the nations" (Isa. 49:6), that God's salvation should reach to the ends of the earth.

Who could believe that God would choose such a servant? Second Isaiah asked. This servant "grew up . . . like a root out of dry ground. He had no form or majesty that we should look at him, nothing in his appearance that we should desire him. He was despised and rejected by others, a man of suffering and acquainted with infirmity; as one from whom others hide their faces he was despised" (Isa. 53:2-3).

"But he was wounded for our transgressions, crushed for our iniquities," Second Isaiah continued; "upon him was the punishment that has made us whole, and by his bruises we are healed" (Isa. 53:5). Israel had long understood the concept of a sacrificial animal's bearing the guilt of a family or community. Second Isaiah took this image a step farther, introducing the striking idea of a sacrificial nation's bearing the guilt of the entire world. "All we like sheep have gone astray, we have all turned to our own way, and the Lord has laid on him the iniquity of us all" (Isa. 53:6).

"It was the will of the Lord to crush him with pain" (Isa. 53:10). Here, Second Isaiah injected a difficult concept, one that countless believers have wrestled with over the years: that God can will suffering. But it was not a senseless, meaningless suffering that Second Isaiah envisioned. "Out of his anguish he shall see light; he shall find satisfaction through his knowledge. The righteous one, my servant, shall make many righteous, and he shall bear their iniquities" (Isa. 53:11).

This theology of Israel as God's servant who suffered so that the world might be redeemed became crucial in the remaining biblical story. In the greatest theological challenge that faced the early church, interpreters turned to Second Isaiah to understand what had happened in the life and death of Jesus of Nazareth.

But even in his own day, this unknown prophet was a powerful voice, painting graphic images of what God was doing in a time when many Israelites still believed that God had abandoned them and gone away.

Our knowledge about the return of Jews to Jerusalem is sketchy. We do know it was not a large-scale migration. Fifty years after they had been exiled, only the oldest had any direct memory of the holy city. Many Jews had created good lives for themselves in Babylon and had no wish to return. Most of those who did made their trek between

538, when Sheshbazzar, a "prince of Judah" (Ezra 1:8), led an initial group, and 520 B.C.E.

For Deliberation

1. Whereas the conquering Babylonians had deported Israel into exile, seeking to prevent them from ever becoming a military threat to Babylon again, the conquering Persians told them to go back home, and to reestablish both their national life and their religion. The one policy implied contempt for those conquered, the other respect. Why do you think Cyrus, the Persian king, would have found this latter policy beneficial to his rule?

2. George Frederick Handel opened his famous oratorio, the *Messiah,* with the words of Isaiah 40:1-5. Handel, in other words, began Christ's story with God's people in exile, in the darkness of bondage, and then proclaimed the glorious good news of God's grace. In contrast, many Christian sermons through the years have begun with a description of the evils we human beings do and then proclaimed the need for us to repent. Compare these two. If you were telling the story of the Messiah and his relation to us, where would you begin?

3. Describe a modern situation in which the proclamation of Isaiah 40:31 would convey great power and hope.

4. Isaiah 52:13–53:12 seems to say that God chooses people of little promise or renown, by earthly standards, to bring about great redemptive consequences. Name a modern instance where this has happened.

15

Reconstitution and Beyond

The Jerusalem temple was rebuilt and rededicated in 516, but as the context was different, so was its significance. With permanent Jewish settlements in Babylon, in Egypt, and in other locations, something besides the temple and the holy city of Jerusalem would have to unite God's people. That something was "the law," the written book of God's instruction. The law became the symbol of God's presence. It provided to Jews a portability that would sustain their identity wherever they went. Jerusalem would continue to occupy a central place in the Israelite heart, and the temple would still be the great holy place of God, but communion with God, relationship with God, the presence of God could now be found through the community's scriptures. This reverence for its sacred writings would remain central to the Jewish religion for centuries to come.

The Bible's story passes over most of the next five hundred years. During this time, Israel was dominated by foreign powers: Persia from 539 to 333, Greece from 333 to 63, and Rome beyond 63 B.C.E. On the whole, this was experienced as an era of God's silence. No outstanding leader arose to deliver the nation from foreign rule. Few prophets spoke compellingly the word of God. Prayers for God's intervention in the nation's destiny seemed mostly unanswered.

Pleas for relief from foreign subjugation rose to heaven and evaporated.

Nevertheless, life went on, and some of the important events of this period are chronicled in the books of Ezra and Nehemiah. Nehemiah supervised the rebuilding of Jerusalem's walls sometime in the latter portion of the fifth century B.C.E. He enjoyed the support of the Persian king, Artaxerxes, in this endeavor, but faced the opposition of local Persian governors, who sought to portray his efforts as insurrection.

During this same time, a priest named Ezra helped Israel complete the transition that made the law the center of Jewish faith. Ezra, who had formerly resided in a Jewish community in Babylonia, brought "the book of the law of Moses" to Jerusalem and read it aloud in public. The document he read probably resembled closely the first five books of our current Bible: Genesis, Exodus, Leviticus, Numbers, and Deuteronomy, subsequently called the Torah. The people of Jerusalem were smitten in conscience by the reading. Ezra led them in celebrating the ancient festival of thanksgiving, the Feast of Tabernacles, and the people entered a solemn covenant to be true to the law of Moses.

Ezra also oversaw a rigorous reform and purification in Israel. Foreign practices and influences were declared corrupt, and Israel was bidden to dedicate itself to purity under the law. The people bound themselves to cease work on the Sabbath, to let agricultural lands lie fallow, and to set aside debt collection every seventh year. The most stringent reform was the vow made by some Israelite men to end marriages with foreign wives and to send away all children of such marriages. The extent to which these reforms were carried out is difficult to gauge.

During this same time, what today we call the Book of Psalms became the hymnbook of the Jerusalem temple. These poetic utterances were far more the words of the faithful spoken to God than the words of God spoken to the faithful. The Psalms developed numerous themes: how suffering and injustice can be so prominent in God's world, the need for God to forget human iniq-

PURIFICATION MOVEMENTS

Efforts to morally cleanse a human community have happened many times through the history of religious faith. Faithful people become horrified at what they perceive as their community's moral degradation, usually in the sphere of sexual behavior, drunkenness, or dishonesty. They believe that God is deeply offended by people who engage in such things. And they imagine how great God's vengeance will be. Sometimes, as with Ezra, such people become prophets of reform, who call the community to a different way of life. Other times, however, such people believe it is their duty to administer God's anger, using whatever power they possess to cleanse the territory, hoping to make God happy. The cleansing can be ruthless, a violence waged in God's name far worse than the evil it supposedly cures.

Later in the biblical story, a follower of God will arise who will entirely recast this cleansing tendency, urging reform among his disciples — but reform undertaken with love and humility, like a king who is also a servant.

uity, God's steadfast love in the midst of adversity, God's royal rule over the entire creation, the beauty and peacefulness of God's holy city, Jerusalem.

There were apparently many hundreds of psalms written; our Bible includes only one hundred fifty.

Probably the most beloved is Psalm 23: "Yea, though I walk through the valley of the shadow of death, I will fear no evil, for Thou art with me." Faithful people throughout the centuries have murmured those words as they approached a difficult time, finding in the ancient words confidence and strength.

Also a favorite is Psalm 100, "Make a joyful noise to the Lord, all the earth!" The psalm bids faithful people to worship together, sing-

AROUND THE WORLD

The Greek philosopher and educator Socrates lived from approximately 469 to 399 B.C.E. Socrates taught that knowledge leads people to act correctly, that it is ignorance that creates evil.

The Greek philosopher and educator Plato lived from approximately 427 to 347 B.C.E. Plato is famous for his dialogues, literary dramas which depicted characters who presented opposing sides of philosophical issues. Socrates, Plato's teacher, was a prominent figure in many of these dialogues.

The Greek philosopher, ethicist, educator, and scientist Aristotle, Plato's student, lived from 384 to 322 B.C.E. He stands as one of the most influential thinkers in the entire history of Western culture, having developed the system of logic that bears his name.

In 338 B.C.E., the first Roman coins were minted.

ing the joyous praises of God so that the entire creation shall hear the proclamation!

In 332 B.C.E., Alexander the Great placed the land of Israel under Greek control. This was at the beginning of the great Hellenistic period, in which, thanks to Alexander's conquests, Greek culture would spread across the entire Middle East. Two Hellenistic dynasties, the Greco-Egyptian Ptolemies or the Syria-based Seleucids, would rule Israel for the next 170 years.

From 175 to 163 B.C.E., Israel was governed by a particularly stringent Greek ruler, Antiochus IV, who called himself Antiochus Epiphanes, a name whose Greek meaning implies that he thought of himself as a god. On taking the throne, Antiochus adopted policies that quickly drove the Jews into outright rebellion. Wanting cultural uniformity among his subjects, he set out to Hellenize them all. A

gymnasium was established in Jerusalem and young men were en-
rolled in it. (Since athletes participated in Greek sports naked, more
than a few young Jews were shamed by their circumcision and under-
went surgery to hide it.) Greek sports were inseparable from Greek
religion, and the presence of a gymnasium in the Holy City was nearly
as offensive to Israel as that of a Greek temple would have been.
Antiochus looted the Jewish temple of its sacred furniture and ves-
sels and even stripped the gold leaf from its facade. But the worst was
yet to come: in 167, Antiochus installed an altar to Zeus in the Jerusalem temple and sacrificed swine there. He then put to death a number
of Jews who refused to touch unclean food. The Jewish people re-
ferred to this as "the abomination of desolation."

The Book of Daniel was penned during this terrible time. Set during the time of Babylonian captivity and revolving around a man of

AROUND THE WORLD

In Greece during the third century B.C.E. a mathematician
named Euclid was laying the foundations for modern geometry and setting up the basic three-dimensional construct by
which the physical world would be understood and analyzed
for more than two thousand years. The story was told that
when the king of Greece asked Euclid for a simple way to understand his work, Euclid replied, "There is no royal road to
geometry."

In 220 B.C.E., construction of the Great Wall of China was
completed under Qin Shi Huangdi. The wall, which measured
4,470 miles, was an effort to keep out the destitute and starv-
ing nomadic Xiong-nu people.

In 217 B.C.E., Hannibal's elephants besieged Rome. The
Carthaginian army drove Roman Legion forces into Lake
Trasimenus where 15,000 died. Two nearby towns are now
named Ossaia ("boneyard") and Sanguineto ("bloodied").

God named Daniel, it urged faithful Jews to remain steadfast through the fires of persecution, in the faith that God remained the author of life and would vindicate the devout.

It was also in this time that a Jew named Mattathias in the village of Modein led his five sturdy sons into the surrounding hills and, joining with other rebels, began waging guerrilla attacks against the Greeks, harrying them, killing them, and destroying pagan religious sites. Mattathias, advanced in years, died within a few months, but his third son, Judas, called "Maccabeus," which meant "the hammer," took up the charge. A recklessly courageous and magnificently gifted young man, Judas Maccabeus turned the resistance into a full-scale struggle for independence. He routed two initial Greek efforts to put down his uprising. Then, when Antiochus sent in a major force, Judas, hopelessly outnumbered, seized the initiative by attacking the enemy camp. He achieved a smashing victory. When Antiochus sent an even larger force, Judas surprised them in their advance and administered a crushing defeat. He then marched triumphantly into Jerusalem, overcoming the Greek garrison stationed there and cleansing the desecrated temple. All items associated with the cult of Zeus were removed. A new altar was erected and dedicated with feasting and great joy. Those who cleansed the temple are said to have found only a single cruse of oil for relighting the holy lamps. The cruse, however, provided oil for eight days, the entire period of dedication. This moment of freedom and triumph continues to be remembered among Jews in the festival of Hanukkah, which is alternately called the Festival of Dedication (*Hanukkah* means *dedication*) or the Festival of Lights. These adventures are chronicled in the Book of 1 Maccabees, a book accepted as scripture by Catholic and Orthodox Christians, but considered useful history, although not scripture, by Protestant Christians and Jews.

Reaching forward from the time of Judas Maccabeus, Israel enjoyed a modest measure of independence. Its Greek overlords were weakened, and the land was at least nominally ruled by the Hasmonean

Jewish dynasty. There were even periods of relative prosperity. The Hasmonean dynasty, however, was rife with internal squabbling, fathers and mothers and sons and brothers fighting with one another for power.

This was the situation in Israel as Rome rose to prominence across the Mediterranean world. Having come to control the entire Italian peninsula, and having overcome its great rival, Carthage, in the three Punic Wars, Rome advanced eastward. In 63 B.C.E., the Roman military leader Pompey allied with the Jewish faction led by Hyrcanus to overthrow Jerusalem's ruling elite, a group led by Hyrcanus's brother Aristobulus. From this moment forward, Israel became a vassal state of Rome. It would continue under Roman dominance throughout the New Testament period, the Roman presence in Palestine being an enormous factor in all that happened in the life of Jesus of Nazareth.

In Rome, Julius Caesar was assassinated by Brutus in 44 B.C.E. Mark Antony carried on his historic love affair with Cleopatra of Egypt which ended in the suicide of both. And Octavian, the future Caesar Augustus, overcame the forces of Antony in civil war and became the first emperor of Rome in 27 B.C.E.

In 37 B.C.E., Rome appointed a half-Jew, Herod, to rule as king of Israel. Herod, a classic tyrant, was a talented, if unprincipled, leader with grandiose ambitions that would eventually cause him to be called Herod the Great. Many of his Jewish subjects, whom he taxed heavily and drove into slave labor, thought of him less generously.

Herod sided with Mark Antony in his contest with Octavian, but adroitly switched sides when Octavian prevailed. In the years that followed, Herod used his considerable skill to court the friendship of Caesar Augustus. He went to great lengths, usually employing sheer intimidation and force, to pacify his Jewish subjects, keeping their urge to rebel in check so that Rome would not be bothered. He engaged in massive building projects all across Israel, one of which, the town of Caesarea (named in honor of Caesar Augustus), was a Roman-style community complete with Roman architecture, stone streets lined with statues of Caesar, and a large amphitheater for Ro-

CICERO

On December 7, 43 B.C.E., Cicero, considered to be one of the greatest statesmen Rome ever produced, was assassinated on orders from Mark Antony for having supported Pompey over the victorious Caesar. A renowned orator, Cicero also translated numerous Greek works so that they might be read and enjoyed by his fellow Romans. In his last work, *On Duties,* he proposed a single solution to all social problems: "Always do the right thing . . . , that which is legal . . . , that which is honest, open and fair, . . . keeping your word, . . . telling the truth, . . . and treating everyone alike."

man entertainment. In the year 12 B.C.E., Herod displayed his love for athletics by underwriting the Olympic games in Greece, and he was named the games' "perpetual president." He built for himself in Jerusalem a splendid royal palace containing immense banquet halls, lavish bedchambers, walls decorated with rare stones, and silver and gold ornaments.

Herod seems also to have suffered from a great deal of paranoia, a condition that grew worse as he aged. In 29 B.C.E., he executed his most beloved wife, Mariamne, suspecting her of adultery. For a time afterward, he became severely depressed and turned to heavy drinking. But when Alexandra, his mother-in-law, tried to seize power, Herod quickly recovered and had her put to death as well. In the latter years of his rule, he executed two of his sons whom he suspected of plotting against him. In 5 B.C.E., Herod became seriously ill and had to be carried about on a couch. Learning that a third son was plotting to take over power, however, he rallied himself and had that son executed. Hearing about all this, Caesar Augustus is said to have remarked, "I would sooner be Herod's pig than his son." Herod died in 4 B.C.E., leaving his kingdom to be divided among his three surviving sons.

FOR DELIBERATION

1. Sometimes when a community of religious people becomes aghast at the moral degradation around them, they will isolate themselves, trying to live a righteous, pure life out on the edge of society. They expect that God will soon rain down judgment on the degradation, and they want to be exempt. Qumran, the ancient site fifteen miles east of Jerusalem where the Dead Sea Scrolls were found, was just such an effort. Considerable attention at Qumran was devoted to ritual purification. Name present-day analogies, groups that have pulled off to the edge of modern society to escape moral decay and live pure lives before God. What are the virtues in such efforts? What are the dangers?

2. Judging by several psalms you know, what are some of the most frequent prayers we pray to God? You might consider Psalm 22, Psalm 51, Psalm 65, Psalm 91, or Psalm 139.

3. What do you think Antiochus IV Epiphanes was trying to accomplish in Israel, and why? (What he in fact accomplished was outright rebellion and defeat!) If you had been one of his royal advisers, what would you have wanted to say to him?

4. What would you think were the main factors that made Judas Maccabeus so effective at winning military engagements with small numbers of troops?

5. Herod is known by history as Herod the Great, mostly because he kept Rome from besieging Israel during his thirty-three-year rule and because he built lavish monuments to himself all over his land. He was called "the half-breed" by his own people because he was the son of a mixed marriage and because his national policies were brutal and repressive. What other national leaders can you think of who were highly regarded across the world yet disdained by their own people?

16

King of the Jews

In 4 B.C.E., stargazers in the east, seeing a brilliant light in the night sky, came to Jerusalem asking where the king of the Jews had been born. In 4 B.C.E., shepherds abiding in the fields, keeping watch over their flocks by night, were visited by a heavenly multitude that sang glad tidings of great joy. In 4 B.C.E., King Herod was told that a "king of the Jews" had been born in his realm. He instructed his soldiers to kill every male child two years old and under in the region where the birth was reported. Herod disliked competition. In 4 B.C.E., God acted, causing a young virgin in the backwater Galilean town of Naza-

---

DECEMBER 25

The Bible does not tell us the actual date of Jesus' birth. We celebrate it on December 25 because, after the Roman Empire became officially Christian in the fourth century C.E., the Romans needed to replace the pagan holiday called the Feast of the Unconquered Sun with a Christian celebration.

---

reth to become pregnant and to bear a son while she and her by-then-husband, Joseph, were in Bethlehem to register for the tax census.

All of these things would have happened in the year 1 C.E., placing the birth of Christ at the beginning of a new age of history, except that the sixth-century C.E. monk, Dionysius Exiguus, who established the dating of the Julian calendar that now guides the Western world, missed his reckoning of Christ's birth by about four years.

WHAT HAPPENED TO THE YEAR ZERO?

The calendar by which we measure time skips from 1 B.C.E. to 1 C.E. There is no year zero. Why not? "Zero," as a concept, was not developed until relatively late in humanity's experience, sometime between 600 and 800 C.E. It remained obscure because all other numbers in the numerical scale designate "something," while zero designates "nothing." It is, therefore, qualitatively different. Zero was probably first identified as a number by Hindu thinkers. Numerous calendars, including the Julian calendar on which our current calendar is based, were in use long before the concept of zero was developed, so that it was never incorporated into them.

When you and I assemble our Christmas crèches replete with shepherds and wise men and angels and sheep and glistening star, we place Jesus' birth in a quiet pastoral setting that implies that the whole world lay gently anticipating his coming. The actual fact could not have been more contrary. Jesus was born into what one observer called a "seething cauldron," a raucous, divisive time in a violent place.

Hundreds, thousands of Roman troops occupied Palestine: haughty, cocky young men whose least interest lay in offering cordiality and respect to the locals. These abiding marauders were accompanied by a far greater number of support personnel: wives, concubines, children, servants, slaves, merchants, moneylenders, black market artists — all of whom felt free to despoil the local population of both its resources and its dignity.

In like manner, the officials Rome sent to govern the region were mostly interested in advancing their own wealth, in furthering their career status, and in keeping the lid on. Quick to plunder the population, they aroused frequent confrontations. Unfortunately, Rome's main tactic for dealing with problems in the region was to send more Roman officials to join the ones already there. It is not difficult to assess how many problems this solved.

Yet not all problems came from the outside. Serious class conflicts divided the Israelite population. Famine, drought, and war had caused many of the less well-off to lose both land and property, driving them into the eager hands of the moneylenders. In 66 C.E., revolutionaries would burn the public archives in an effort to erase debt records. Urban priests and rural priests were in open conflict. The high priesthood in Jerusalem lived a lavish lifestyle, collaborating with Rome to maintain their own fortunes, while often sending thugs to rob the poorer country priests of their tithes. Class banditry was commonplace. Robin Hoods of the ancient world pillaged those with possessions.

And then there were the revolutionaries. Some vengeful, angry, hot-headed man, determined to bring the power of his manhood against the hated Romans, would gather around him a band of disciples, remove them to a secluded place in the Judean hills, train them in savage warfare, and lead them in raids against the Roman garrison in a nearby town or village. The memory of Judas Maccabeus undoubtedly inspired more than a few. The main thing these "men of the dagger" (as they would later be known) accomplished was to bring the wrath of Rome against a Jewish population that was expected to cooperate in zealot extermination. Thousands of people suffered and died, and the powerful Romans were not in the least measure expelled. But the zealotry continued.

This was the world of the young Jesus of Nazareth: a hard, dangerous setting of class division, exploitation, poverty, greed, and frequent bloodshed. Undoubtedly present as well among common people were love, tenderness, community, caring, and self-sacrifice —

these things are nearly always found in human populations — but the public picture was one of massive unrest.

We know very little about Jesus' childhood. He was born in Bethlehem. He grew up in the town of Nazareth, several miles southwest of the Sea of Galilee. His father was a carpenter. He had younger brothers and sisters.

The region where he spent his youth, Galilee, was known in Jerusalem as coarse and unseemly, mostly because of the large number of Gentiles who lived there. Jesus' disciple Nathanael's comment, "Can anything good come out of Nazareth?" expressed a common sentiment about the region. But, just as God had previously reached into Egypt and selected to relate to lowly slaves, so God now reached into uncouth Galilee and began this new work with a peasant baby.

We see in this dynamic what will become a very prominent New Testament pattern. The challenge faced by New Testament writers was to proclaim that God had acted again, powerfully, in their time. There was widespread agreement among Jews that God had acted in ancient times, in Egypt at the Red Sea, in giving Israel the Promised Land, in speaking through the prophets. Believers agreed on that. The New Testament issue was whether God had acted again in the first century, and whether the records of these acts deserved to be sacred texts. The main method New Testament writers chose for making their case was to claim that God had essentially done the very same thing God had done before. Just as God worked through a slave child, Moses, in Pharaoh's domain, God had now worked through a blue-collar baby, Jesus, in Caesar's domain. Just as God had delivered a tortured, embattled people to freedom and wholeness beyond the Red Sea, God had now created out of the tortured embattlement of first-century Palestine a new community of freedom and wholeness. This claim — that what God did formerly God has done again in our time — is the fundamental pattern in which the New Testament is constructed.

Raised in Galilee, Jesus came forward as a man of about thirty, preaching that "the kingdom of God" was dawning and that God's

TWO TESTAMENTS

I hear frequently the characterization that the Old Testament portrays a God of anger and vengeance, while the New Testament portrays a God of love and compassion, and that the Bible would be a better book with just the New Testament.

I urge my readers not to think this way. There is just as much divine vengeance in the New Testament as in the Old, and just as much divine love in the Old Testament as in the New. The New Testament loses its meaning without the Old Testament; its roots are ripped away. It is not understood as part of the ongoing drama of God's redeeming purpose.

The New Testament is not an "improvement" on the Old, superseding it with a "higher" faith. Christianity is not an "improvement" on Judaism, superseding it as a "higher" religion. Christians and Jews are inextricably bound members of the same family who do not agree on everything even though they arise from the same source — the almighty Creator who loves both dearly.

people should repent in preparation. He gathered twelve disciples and spent considerable time instructing and training them. They traveled together the region of Galilee in northern Israel where Jesus healed people of their illnesses and afflictions and taught those who followed him. He gained a considerable reputation in the area. After nearly three years, he and his disciples traveled southward to Jerusalem, the holy city. Before a week had passed, the reigning powers in Jerusalem had decided to eliminate him. They thought him to be a lawbreaker and a sinner. It is likely that they also thought him to be another self-appointed zealot intent on striking at the Romans and gaining power for himself. He was arrested. His disciples, who had pledged their allegiance through whatever happened, fled. One of them, Peter, denied three times that he had ever known Jesus. Jesus was tried, convicted, and sentenced to die by crucifixion, the Romans' preferred style of capital punishment for common criminals. He was crucified the same afternoon, nails in his hands, and he died. He was buried in a tomb, a small cave in the ground, as was customary. A large stone was placed over the entrance.

Two days later, women went early in the morning to place spices in the tomb as an act of mourning. They found the stone rolled away. Entering the tomb, they encountered a Presence who told them Jesus had been raised from the dead and was no longer there. The accounts of what the women did then vary greatly. According to Luke, the women ran back to the disciples in great awe to tell them. The disciples discounted the story at first, thinking it a typical product of excitable females. But one disciple, Peter, decided to check for himself. He, too, found the tomb empty as the women had said.

In the days ahead, the risen Christ appeared repeatedly to the disciples, commissioning them to continue his work and promising that he, in the Spirit, would be with them. Many times that happened. Then his Spirit, on the Day of Pentecost, came to a group of his followers and empowered them to preach strongly in different languages. His Spirit empowered Peter, who had betrayed Jesus at his crucifixion, to speak boldly to a crowd in Jerusalem. His Spirit brought unity to the believers who gathered to follow him. His Spirit empowered another one of his followers, Stephen, to testify before the Jerusalem Council and to remain faithful even unto death by stoning. His Spirit confronted the great persecutor of Christians, a young Pharisee named Saul, on the road to Damascus and converted him into Paul, the great missionary for Christ to the Gentile world. His Spirit caused churches to spring up in many towns and cities across the Mediterranean world in response to Paul's preaching. His Spirit continues to live in and invigorate the church, even unto the present time. For where two or three gather in Christ's name, his Spirit is in the midst of them.

FOR DELIBERATION

1. Ponder the notion of God's becoming human. It is an enormous contradiction. A great mystery. But the greater mystery is that God became human not in a king who wielded power, but in a peasant child who possessed no power, not in the strength of dominance but in the weakness of humility. What shall we make of this? How are we to respond?

2. Why would God come amid chaos, turmoil, violence, suffering, and death, rather than into a peaceful, pastoral setting? What does it mean if God continues to do the same thing now?

3. Who do you think crucified Jesus? Can you concur with hymn-writer Johann Heermann, who wrote in the famous hymn "Ah, Holy Jesus": "Who was the guilty? Who brought this upon You? It was my treason, Lord, that has undone You. 'Twas I, Lord Jesus, I it was denied you; I crucified you"? How do you and I crucify Jesus?

4. James Sanders has said, "If your reading of a biblical text causes you to feel self-righteous, you can be absolutely certain that you are misinterpreting the text." How have Christians misinterpreted the story of Christ's crucifixion to make us feel self-righteous?

17

The Gospel of Matthew

Accounts of His Life

The New Testament begins with four accounts of Jesus' life: the Gospels of Matthew, Mark, Luke, and John. Each is both a report and an interpretation of Jesus' ministry, death, and resurrection. The editors who compiled the New Testament apparently gave us four pictures of Jesus instead of just one in an effort to convey a more complete portrait. Just as God is far bigger than any one theology, so Christ is far bigger than any one gospel. We need to see him from several vantage points to get a sense of who he was.

If this seems strange, think of how it is true of other historical figures as well. For example, if I want an accurate picture of Thomas Jefferson I will read several biographies, plus books that provide the eighteenth-century context. After this I will begin to piece together my perception of who Thomas Jefferson really was. So with Jesus.

The purpose of these gospel accounts was to create disciples. To claim those of us who read them as followers of Christ. To make it possible for us who live in a later time to hear the same call heard by the original twelve — "Follow me!" — and to discern what following him will mean. The gospels should therefore be thought of, first and foremost, as *sermons,* efforts to convince, attempts to change you and me and make us different people. If we do not hear through these writings a clear and compelling call, we have missed the point.

GOSPEL GENRE

The gospels are not primarily history, although they have plenty of history in them. The gospels are not primarily biography, even though they report many details from the life of Jesus of Nazareth. The gospels are not primarily law or instruction, even though Jesus' teachings are prominent. The gospels are *sermons,* written to create disciples. When we read the Bible, we need to struggle hard to hear what the writers *were trying to say,* not what they *were not trying to say*! The gospels were written to convince us, to claim us.

The four gospels differ in many respects, as we will see in a moment, but they also agree fundamentally. Their major agreement is that Jesus, an unknown peasant who essentially came out of nowhere, was Israel's king sent by God. All four gospels tell his story around a specific pattern, the order of an ancient coronation procession. Coronation processions usually consisted of four elements. (1) A proclaimer walked at the head of the procession, announcing that the king-to-be-crowned was coming and calling the gathered throngs to humble themselves before him. In the gospels, John the Baptist is the proclaimer. (2) Evidences of his power were exhibited for all to see, usually the booty of his conquests. In the gospels, Jesus' healings, his teachings, his signs and wonders are set forth. (3) The coming king appears, typically atop his great steed, amid great acclaim. In the gospels, Jesus rides a donkey, along a carpet of leafy branches, with the throng shouting, "Hosanna! Blessed is he who comes in the name of the Lord! Hosanna in the highest!" (4) The crown to be placed on the king's head is borne by religious priests, and the king is lifted up on high amid the people. In the gospels, a crown is indeed placed on his head, and he is lifted up.

Modern readers are not conditioned to see this symbolism, but to an ancient reader, the message would have been clear: God was crowning a king! A new realm was being established. But the anomalies would also have been clear: the crown was a crown of thorns, not jewels. The lifting up was upon a cross, not a throne. The final acclamation was derision and insult, not reverence. The end was suffering and death, not power and might. The people hated him, treated him as a criminal; yet God worked through these human acts to crown and exalt him king. We were doing one thing; God, through the same events, was doing something else. We meant evil; God used our evil for good, to save us. Do you recall the story of Joseph and his brothers?

On this message, all four gospels agree. Beyond this, they diverge widely, giving us a rich and multi-dimensional picture of the one the Gospel of John calls the Word made flesh. Far from trying to resolve the differences between their pictures, our opportunity is to include all four into our image of the one who calls us.

Matthew's Gospel

The Gospel of Matthew presents Jesus as the new Moses, the giver of God's new law to the new Israel.

Jesus, according to Matthew, was born to Mary and Joseph while Herod was King of Israel. Astrologers from the east, non-Israelites, saw a brilliant star that led them to his birthplace, revealing to them that a king had been born. Just as the infant Moses had been born under threat from Pharaoh in Egypt, so the infant Jesus was born under threat from King Herod. As Moses' mother had hidden her baby among bulrushes on the Nile, so Mary and Joseph hid their baby by escaping to Egypt until Herod's death. Just as Moses had climbed Mt. Sinai to deliver the law, so also Jesus climbed the mountain by the Sea of Galilee to deliver the new law. As Moses had addressed to his people the Ten Commandments and the covenant code, Jesus ad-

"THE BEGATS"

When reading the Bible, we modern believers often skip over "the begats," the genealogies. Matthew, however, begins his gospel (Matt. 1:2-16) with a genealogy we do well to notice because of its distinct message. Matthew lists forty generations of fathers and sons from Abraham to Jesus. He also lists, however, five women: Tamar (mistress of Judah), Rahab (wife of Salmon), Ruth (wife of Boaz), "the wife of Uriah" (Bathsheba, mistress and then wife of David), and Mary (wife of Joseph). Four of these five "mothers of Jesus," all of them but Mary, were foreigners, women from other nations. Matthew was apparently very struck by the circuitous route God took in fulfilling the promises to Abraham, through Jews and Gentiles, believers and unbelievers, the faithful and the heathen. Through males, Matthew expressed God's fidelity to Abraham's lineage. Through females, he expressed God's surprises, God's creativity, God's freedom. You and I might have to stretch our minds and our faiths to acknowledge that one of Jesus' grandmothers, Rahab, was a Canaanite prostitute. God doesn't do things the way we specify!

dressed to his people the Sermon on the Mount (Matt. 5–7). As Moses had delivered the old law written upon tablets of stone, Jesus delivered the new law to be written upon the heart.

Matthew proclaimed that in Jesus Christ God had brought to earth a new way of living, a new ethic. It was the way Moses had previously brought, except more so. "Do not think that I have come to abolish the law and the prophets," he recorded Jesus telling the people, "I have come not to abolish but to fulfill. For truly I tell you, until heaven and earth pass away, not one letter, not one stroke of a letter, will pass from the law until all is accomplished" (Matt. 5:17-18). Jesus called for rigor, for devotion, for new commitment. But it was not a commitment to legal minutia, as some in Jesus' day practiced. It was a commitment to the spirit of the law. Behind the words written on the scroll was an intention, a purpose, a living design that emanated from the heart of God. To know that purpose, to relate to that heart, Matthew said, was the meaning of the law. "On that day, many will say to me, 'Lord, Lord, did we not prophesy in your name, and cast out demons in your name, and do many deeds of power in your name?' Then I will declare to them, 'I never knew you; go away from me, you evildoers'" (Matt. 7:22-23). The heart of the matter was that "I never knew you." Our knowing God, God's knowing us, that relationship, was the real meaning of God's law. The new Moses brought a law that God would write on the hearts of God's people, so that it would live there forever, creating them, motivating them, guiding their path. This was the law the prophet Jeremiah had anticipated:

> I will put my law within them, and write it upon their hearts; and I will be their God, and they shall be my people. No longer shall they teach one another, or say to each other, "Know the Lord," for they shall all know me, from the least of them to the greatest, says the Lord. (Jer. 31:33-34)

Matthew depicted Jesus as carrying out strenuous arguments over the law with the most devoutly religious people of his day. They criticized him sternly for being a lawbreaker:

> He left that place and entered their synagogue; a man was there with a withered hand, and they asked him, "Is it lawful to cure on the Sabbath?" so that they might accuse him. He said to them, "Suppose one of you has only one sheep and it falls into a pit on the Sabbath; will you not lay hold of it and lift it out? How much more valuable is a human being than a sheep! So it is lawful to do good on the Sabbath." Then he said to the man, "Stretch out your hand." He stretched out his hand, and it was restored, as sound as the other. But the Pharisees went out and conspired against him, how to destroy him. (Matt. 12:9-14)

LAW

Law is a highly ambivalent phenomenon. It can be enormous blessing; it can also be great curse. Law is necessary for a human society to function. If we did not have traffic laws, our cars would not take us far. If we did not have commerce laws, our economy would be a jungle of greed. If we did not have election laws, democracy would mean nothing. Law is necessary to bring order to society and to place boundaries on what we will do against one another, to civilize our behavior.

And, furthermore, we human beings need rigor. We need people who place high expectations on us and motivate us to do the best we can do. Half-hearted devotion yields very little. On the other hand, we badly misuse law. We delude ourselves into believing that if we have followed the law, we have done all that is needed. "I broke no law!" — how many times have those words been spoken to justify greedy, immoral behavior?

People with power can often use laws to serve their own interests and to exploit those for whom they have no concern.

To expect laws from the first century C.E. or the tenth century B.C.E. to provide good ethics and morality in the twenty-first century C.E. is highly problematic. Some ancient laws make good modern ethics, such as, "You shall not steal" (Exod. 20:15). But other ancient laws do not: "You shall not permit a female sorcerer [a witch] to live" (Exod. 22:18) As a famous hymn, "Once to Every Man and Nation," puts it, "Time makes ancient good uncouth."

While law is necessary in our life, and rigor is absolutely necessary in our faith, to reduce life and faith to law is filled with problems. We shall later hear the Apostle Paul make this same point very strongly.

Jesus, according to Matthew, was God's new Moses who proclaimed a new law of the heart, a law that urges us to be rigorous in living in accord with the heart of God.

But he criticized them for focusing on minutia and missing the underlying point.

> Woe to you, scribes and Pharisees, hypocrites! For you tithe mint, dill, and cumin, and have neglected the weightier matters of the law: justice and mercy and faith. It is these you ought to have practiced without neglecting the others. You blind guides! You strain out a gnat but swallow a camel! (Matt. 23:23-24)

Matthew made it clear that the "heart" of the law Jesus delivered consisted of exactly what Amos and Micah and other prophets had said centuries before: doing justice and showing mercy to brothers and sisters in greatest need. "Lord, when was it that we saw you hungry and gave you food, or thirsty and gave you something to drink? Or when was it that we saw you a stranger, and welcomed you, or naked and gave you clothing?" (Matt. 25:37-38). "Truly I tell you, as you did it to one of the least of these who are members of my family, you did it to me" (Matt. 25:40).

To discern God's law faithfully, according to Matthew, was to know God's heart. And God's heart continued to be as it had always been: a heart of great and overwhelming love, especially for the earth's least and lowliest, but also for the least and the lowly in all of us. Jesus, as Matthew told the story, was God's new Moses, sent to call God's people to a right devotion to God's will, a devotion that would restore relationship with the Almighty.

FOR DELIBERATION

1. Identify someone you know on whom you keep getting new insights and perspectives. What have you learned lately that you did not know earlier? How long do you think it will take you to get a full and adequate picture of that person?
2. We noted that the gospels are sermons, written to create disciples. To what have you felt called by God through past readings

from the gospels? What gospel words have particularly spoken to you, and to what have they beckoned you?

3. "God was crowning a king" — the message on which all four gospels agree. In that day, kings were leaders, individuals in whom the people could place absolute trust. In our day, most nations do not have kings. What are some other images that can help us to understand the role God has sent Jesus to play in our lives?

4. "Be perfect . . . , even as your heavenly Father is perfect" (Matt. 5:48). Those words can be an enormous blessing or a wicked curse. Describe the difference.

5. "As you did it to one of the least of these who are members of my family, you did it to me" (Matt. 25:40). If you were writing a sermon on those words of Jesus, whom, around us at the present time, would you name as "the least of these"?

6. *Law* and *relationship* play dual, but sometimes contradictory, roles in creating us as human beings. I have suggested that Matthew wanted to present Jesus as the new Moses, the giver of a new law founded on relationship. Remember your own childhood. What role did law (rules) play in making you the person you have become? Can you remember rules that were particularly determinative for you? What role did human relationships play? Who were the most formative and important people in your life? How would you describe the relative role of each factor? Which was dominant?

18

The Gospel of Mark

The Gospel of Mark presents Jesus as God's servant who remained faithful through the worst persecution and death the world could offer, and who bids us to the same faithfulness.

The Gospel of Mark was written to a persecuted community, to Christians who were suffering because of their faith. This community may have been in Rome, in Galilee, or elsewhere; no one knows. The persecution was so severe, however, that members of the community were tempted day by day to forsake their commitment to Christ. The pressure was enormous. Probably, believers were being arrested, imprisoned, and put to death.

Because of this persecution, one huge question loomed in the Christian community. Jesus had commanded power to do great signs and wonders. He had cast out demons, healed sick people, repaired broken bodies, fed multitudes. Many had been restored by his power. The question the Christians were asking was, "If he delivered them, why doesn't he deliver us? We profess the same faith they did; why doesn't he reach into our affliction and save us?"

Mark filled the first part of his gospel with Jesus' signs and wonders: the exorcism of demons, the restoration of a man's withered hand, the curing of a fever, the stilling of a storm on the sea. But repeatedly, Jesus admonished his followers, "Don't tell anyone!" "Keep it quiet!" "Don't spread the word!" It was not, apparently, by signs and wonders that Jesus wished to be known. He did not come to establish a miracle religion that promised that God would heal anyone who demonstrated sufficient faith.

In the latter portion of Mark's gospel, the passion narrative, Jesus marched resolutely toward his own crucifixion and death. He was arrested. He was examined by the Jerusalem Council. He was questioned by Pontius Pilate, the Roman governor. He was placed, along with a criminal named Barabbas, before a Jerusalem crowd. He was handed over to Roman soldiers for crucifixion. He was nailed to the cross. He suffered. He died. Nowhere did he perform a miracle to save himself. As he hung on the cross, those who passed by challenged him, "Save yourself, and come down from the cross" (Mark 15:30). The chief priests and scribes mocked him, "He saved others; he cannot save himself" (Mark 15:31).

Jesus did not bring down a miracle for his own deliverance. Instead, Jesus remained faithful to God to the end. He did not, despite earth's condemnation and persecution, veer from his commitment. He said to his disciples, "The one who endures to the end will be saved" (Mark 13:13), and then he became the living embodiment of that challenge.

And he thereby called his followers, the church, to remain faithful through their persecution. He called them to stand firmly before the same earthly powers that had tortured him. His persecution and their persecution were of one piece, the called of God being judged by human authority. And the church's destiny would be the same as Christ's: beyond the persecution they would find victory and life. Behind their current turmoils, the hand of God wove a larger purpose.

The Gospel of Mark is a challenge to keep faith through the hot fires of earthly rebuff.

Throughout the ages, the faithful have repeatedly been tempted by miracle religion. Many televangelists seem to specialize in it, and apparently it was around in the ancient world as well. "If you believe strongly enough," this kind of religion goes, "if you believe earnestly enough, in the depths of your heart, then God will heal you. God will restore your blind eye! God will cure your cancer! God will take away your financial burdens! You must have faith!"

The Christ of Mark spoke a resounding "No!" to miracle religion. You cannot manipulate God! You cannot call down healing power! God is far, far beyond your control, not subject to your magic, your incantations. Pray for a miracle, yes. Hope for a miracle, yes. Rejoice if a miracle comes, yes. But put miracles at the center of faith, no! Prove your faith with a miracle, no! Lose your faith if there is no miracle, no!

Christ remained faithful to God through the worst persecution earth could inflict, with no miracle. The Gospel of Mark reminded the early Christians, just as it reminds us today, that Christ calls us to follow him. "The one who endures to the end will be saved."

THE SYROPHOENICIAN WOMAN

Mark tells an especially intriguing story of a time when Jesus journeyed up to the region of Tyre, in Lebanon on the Mediterranean coast (Mark 7:24-30). A Gentile woman, a Syrophoenician, begged him to cast out a demon from her daughter. Jesus replied with a common saying of his day: "Let the children be fed first; it is not fair to take the children's food and throw it to the dogs," meaning, "I am here to heal Israel, not you heathen." Our modern-day version of the saying would be, "Charity begins at home." The woman, however, begging for the restoration of her daughter, said, "Sir, even the dogs under the table eat the children's crumbs," or, "Doesn't God love the whole creation, not just Israel? Isn't your theology a bit confined?" To which Jesus replied, "For that saying, the demon has left your daughter," honoring her resourcefulness and her faith. I once wrote a sermon on this text entitled, "The Gentile Woman Who Preached the Greatness of God to Jesus."

FOR DELIBERATION

1. Through what experience in your life have you had the hardest time maintaining your faith?

2. Read Psalm 22:1-18. When all the results are bad, when life is awful, are you able to shout and complain against God the way this psalmist did? Now read the rest of Psalm 22. How is it that strong complaint can be part of a faithful relationship with God rather than a loss of faith?

3. Why is miracle religion so inviting, so deceptive, and so cruel all at once?

4. Describe someone you know who has endured hardship after hardship and remained faithful to God.

5. "The one who endures to the end will be saved." To some people, this challenge from Mark 13:13 contains little or no "good news," only grueling demand. What good news do you find in it?

19

The Gospel of Luke

The Gospel of Luke presents Jesus as the bearer of God's love to the entire world, not just to Israel. Luke was amazed, exhilarated, that God, in Christ, had chosen to step beyond the boundaries of Israel and to offer redemption to the nations.

Luke alone traced Jesus' genealogy to Adam, the father of all humanity (Luke 3:23-38).

Luke depicted Jesus as blowing the ancient jubilee horn, announcing the great day of the Lord's redemption — but not just in Israel, across the entire world! To many in Israel this reeked of heresy, and Luke tells us that Jesus almost got stoned for it (Luke 4:16-30).

Luke told of a Samaritan, a despised half-breed, who brought the love of God to a beaten man on the Jericho road when a priest and a Levite had not stopped to help (Luke 10:27-37).

Luke related the story of a great dinner given by God. The honored guests, first on the invitation list, all sent excuses saying why they could not attend. So God declared, "Go out . . . into the streets and lanes of the town and bring in the poor, the crippled, the blind and the lame. Go also onto the roads and highways, and compel people to come." And when it was done, the house was completely filled (Luke 14:15-24).

The Book of Acts is a continuation of the Gospel of Luke, written by the same author, and it carries forward the theme of God's redemption of the entire world through Jesus. In it, Luke told of the Day of Pentecost, in which the tongues of Jesus' disciples were empowered to preach the gospel in a multitude of languages to every nation under heaven (Acts 2).

Luke also related the story of Christ's laying claim on the foremost persecutor of Christians, Saul of Tarsus, and commissioning him to be the foremost missionary for Christ across the Mediterranean world (Acts 9). And he told of how the gift of the Holy Spirit came to a Roman military officer and his family, to the disbelief and amazement of the Apostle Peter (Acts 11).

Several themes run through the Gospel of Luke and the Book of Acts, but from just this short selection of vignettes, we can see that this one dominates: all these stories tell of the one who came to push outward the boundaries, to include far more people in the family of faith than the faithful had imagined, to call people in every nation and realm to be bearers of God's love. Luke knew that we faithful people repeatedly try to draw God's boundaries. "We belong to God; they don't," we sometimes say. "God resides with us, true followers; God does not associate with them, unsaved sinners." First-century Israel had established a firm boundary between themselves and the rest of the world.Christians in our time are tempted to do the same thing. More than a few of us see ourselves as God's true followers in a depraved world of sin and error.

God, if we are to believe Luke, will have none of it! God claims followers from many nations, many peoples. God alone determines what in us is righteousness and what is sin. Our guidelines are too small, too limited. God can awaken hearts and people whom you and I have discounted and bring from them genuine devotion.

Luke presents a Christ who offers God's saving redemption far beyond the boundaries set by the faithful, calling us all to vastly enlarge our minds about the size and reach of God's amazing grace.

For Deliberation

1. After Jesus' sermon in the Nazareth synagogue, the worshippers became so angry that they tried to kill him (Luke 4:16-30). This was apparently because he told them that God was blowing the jubilee horn, announcing the great day of God's redemption, not just in Israel but all across the whole world, freeing and claiming people who had not related to God before. How was this an offense to their beliefs, their pride? How does this parallel Luke's story of the elder brother in Luke 15:25-32? What analogies can you find with things going on today?

2. The Book of Jonah in the Old Testament is the story of a prophet who wanted God to hate the same wretched foreigners that Jonah hated: the people of the great tormentor city of Nineveh. When God forgave the people of Nineveh, Jonah did not rejoice; he went outside the city and sulked. Name people in our world we want God to hate. Would we respond any differently from Jonah if God declared forgiveness toward those we hate?

3. Tell of a time when God's love came to you through a person you fully did not expect, someone outside the ranks of the possible.

4. How can we, at one and the same time, believe and cherish our beloved Christian faith but also believe that God can work through people outside our faith?

20

The Gospel of John

The Gospel of John presents Jesus as the one-with-God figure who came to shine light into the world's darkness and show us a path out of that darkness.

The world, to John, was a place of great darkness: "This is the judgment, that the light has come into the world, and people loved darkness rather than light because their deeds were evil" (John 3:19). The darkness is the result of human sin, a condition we long ago inflicted upon ourselves. We human beings need light, direction.

Yet God did not leave the world desolate. According to John, Jesus brought God's light so that all could see and live in the way of truth. "In him was life, and the life was the light of all people. The light shines in the darkness, and the darkness did not overcome it" (John 1:4-5).

God's light shining into the world's darkness was John's dominant metaphor for Jesus: "Jesus spoke to them, saying, 'I am the light of the world. Whoever follows me will never walk in darkness, but will have the light of life" (John 8:12). But John employed other metaphors as well.

"The lamb of God who takes away the sin of the world" (John

1:29). This metaphor finds its meaning in the ancient practice of animal sacrifice as atonement for guilt.

"The savior of the world" (John 4:42). John saw Jesus as the one who could take sinful and broken lives and redirect them toward wholeness. Nowhere is this more clear than in the story of Jesus' conversation with the woman at the well (John 4:1-42).

"The bread of life" (John 6:35). John recounted a time when Jesus fed a crowd of five thousand people with five loaves of barley bread and two fish (John 6:1-14). John's original audience would immediately have recalled how God fed ancient Israel with manna and quail in the wilderness.

"The Word made flesh" (John 1:14). To John, Jesus was the embodiment of the creative power of God, one with God from the beginning, who could make all things new.

"Rivers of living water" (John 7:38). Recalling how God provided Israel with water in the Sinai Desert, this metaphor pictured Jesus as a spring and the Spirit that he would give as flowing water. All who believed in Jesus were invited to drink this water.

"The good shepherd" (John 10:11). In Jesus' day, a hired hand had no vested interest in the sheep entrusted to his care; if danger threatened, he would save himself and let the sheep be scattered. Not so with Jesus. This image would have recalled to John's audience the shepherd of Psalm 23: "The LORD is my shepherd. . ."

"The true vine" (John 15:1). The prophet Isaiah compared Israel to a vine that yielded sour grapes (Isa. 5); John compared Jesus to a vine pruned by God to yield good, sweet grapes.

The primary gift Christ brought to earth, according to John, was God's love. John uses the Greek word *agape*, unconditional, self-sacrificial love, thirty-one times in his gospel, compared to twenty-two uses by Matthew, Mark, and Luke combined. "God so loved the world that he gave his only son . . ." (John 3:16). "I give you a new commandment, that you love one another. Just as I have loved you, you should also love one another. By this will everyone know that you are my disciples, if you have love for one another" (John 13:34-35). "No one has greater love than this, to lay down one's life for one's friends"

(John 15:13). "I made your name known to them, and I will make it known, so that the love with which you have loved me may be in them" (John 17:26). These are just a few of the passages in John's gospel in which love is mentioned.

Jesus also brought to earth a peace that passes all understanding, "Peace I leave with you; my peace I give to you. I do not give to you as the world gives. Do not let your hearts be troubled, and do not let them be afraid" (John 14:27).

The Gospel of John is replete with exquisite language, memorable quotes. No gospel has been memorized and repeated more by Christians. For this reason it can easily be interpreted as a set of worthy ideals we all need to believe in, lofty goals for our spiritual devotion, the kind of thing everyone affirms but no one actually does. But John forbade his readers to view his book that way. "Feed my lambs," Jesus says to his disciple Peter at the end of the story (John 21:15). "Tend my sheep" (John 21:16). "Feed my sheep" (John 21:17). These words are a call to action. John was saying to his readers, "Immerse yourself in the messy, ambivalent, demanding business of caring about people. Devote yourself to the human struggle around you." The Gospel of John was not a call to lofty ideals. It was a call to realize that the loftiest one of all became human and took part in our plight: feeding hungry people, curing illnesses, confronting the manipulative, self-serving powers of his day. This is how the light shines into the darkest corners, and the darkness is not able to overcome it.

In the gospels we have four pictures of one Christ: Christ who came to write the law of God upon our hearts, Christ who bids us to remain faithful through the worst of the world's persecutions, Christ who offers God's love and redemption to all humanity, Christ who shines the light of God into the deepest recesses of our darkened world. The four pictures provide great richness, a full picture of the discipleship to which Christ calls us.

FOR DELIBERATION

1. Which of John's metaphors for Jesus — light of the world, lamb of God, savior, bread of life, Word made flesh, rivers of living water, good shepherd, true vine — do you find most meaningful in your life? Why?

2. If we preach that Jesus gives "a peace that passes all understanding," what is the power in that message? What is the danger; how can we misuse it?

3. The Greek dialect in which the New Testament was written has three different words which are translated into English by the word "love." *Eros* denotes strong desire, creative love, often sexual drive. *Philia* denotes friendship, amiability, neighborly love, as in philanthropy. (*Philadelphia* means "city of brotherly love.") *Agape* is spiritual, self-giving, self-sacrificial love. Describe a person you know of who has exemplified *philia*. Dr. Martin Luther King, Jr., preached a very powerful sermon on these three Greek words; what would you imagine he said? As you would estimate it, how much of each of these three types of love needs to be present in a good marriage? In a good human community?

21

The Resurrection

All four gospels report that death could not hold him. After Jesus lived among us, after he was condemned by the religious and civil authorities, after he was crucified, after he died and his body was placed in a tomb, all four gospels announce that the tomb was found empty. The stone that guarded it was rolled away. He was gone. This might have been deception or robbery — then as now, many suspected as much — except that his followers began experiencing his renewed presence in unexpected times and places. He talked with them. He fed them meals. He beckoned them into God's service. His spirit enlivened in them conviction and boldness. The early church was awed and exhilarated at finding the spirit of the risen Christ continuing in their midst. They especially found him present when they broke bread and drank wine together, as he had told them to do, in what would become the sacrament of the Lord's Supper.

As God had first reached into Egypt and brought an enslaved people to freedom, God now reached into the greatest enslavement of all, the grave, and wrought a new freedom. As God had long ago conquered Israel's enemies round about, God now conquered the most formidable enemy of all. This, according to the Bible, is the character of God: to take a tiny mustard seed and create a great plant, to take the smallest possibilities and create huge outcomes, to take the captivity of a sealed tomb and create a living presence that will change the world. "Is anything impossible for God?" an angel had asked Abraham (Gen. 18:14). Answering across the ages, another angel said to Mary, "No, nothing is impossible for God" (Luke 1:37).

God re-creates! God brings life from death! God can begin with the driest bones and fill them with living vigor!

You have to be a bit naïve to believe this. All good sense denies it. No analysis will figure it out. No deduction will lead to it. No experiment can show how it is done. It is absurdity to any sound-thinking child of the Enlightenment.

But it is the message of Easter morning, a proclamation that invites not scientific analysis but awestruck wonder. The theologian Karl Barth once said that Christian believers arrive for Sabbath worship asking one question beneath all others — "Is it really true?" — and hoping against all odds that it is. Can the battered and broken remains of a used-up life rise and find fresh vigor? If not, we are doomed; if so, we are victorious! We human beings need this promise if we are to continue forward. "The trumpet shall sound, and the dead shall be raised . . . ! Thanks be to God who gives us this victory through our Lord Jesus Christ" (1 Cor. 15:52, 57).

FOR DELIBERATION

1. What causes you to be skeptical about resurrection? Why do you believe in it?
2. Tell of a person you have seen "raised from the dead."
3. Describe instances in which you have seen the spirit of the resurrected Christ working in or among people in our time.
4. In the quote from 1 Corinthians 15 above, Paul implies that the central motivation behind a Christian life is *awe* followed by *thanksgiving*. Name some other motivations that Christians sometimes preach, like *fear*, or *desire for reward*, or *the requirement of purity*. What primary factor do you want motivating your life as a believer?

22

The Early Church

At the beginning of his ministry, Jesus had gathered around him twelve disciples. They received his instructions and teaching. They accompanied him on his journeys. They performed healings and other acts of compassion in his name. They ate and drank with him, witnessing all that he said and did. They were present when he was arrested. He appeared to them, once, twice, more, after God raised him from the dead. They came to understand, as few others, that this man was, in some mysterious way, God incarnate, sent to call a lost humanity back to the way the Creator intended.

One day not long after Jesus' resurrection, his disciples were gathered together in Jerusalem, in the home of one of his followers. Suddenly, a sound came from heaven like the rush of a mighty wind. It filled the entire house. The Spirit that was in the wind claimed them, their minds, their hearts, their mouths, their tongues, for God's service. All of them were filled with a strong and compelling passion, and they began to speak in many tongues.

In diverse languages they were able to proclaim God's deeds of power. Devout Jews from many nations were living in Jerusalem at the time, as were many non-Jews. All of them were amazed to hear simple Galileans preaching in their native languages. From this mo-

> ### *RUACH*
>
> It is important to know that in ancient Hebrew culture, "wind" and "spirit" were the same concept, represented by the same word, *ruach*. A strong gust of wind meant that a spirit was present.

ment, the gospel of Jesus Christ would reach out to the nations and bring from every people and family those God called to discipleship. This day, fifty days after Jesus' resurrection, became known as Pentecost (Acts 2:1-13).

The disciple Peter addressed the crowd that witnessed this happening, proclaiming boldly that God had raised Jesus from the dead and made him Lord and Messiah. About three thousand people welcomed his message that day and were baptized. "They devoted themselves to the apostles' teaching and fellowship, to the breaking of bread and the prayers" (Acts 2:42). Thus did new believers begin to associate with what was first called "the Way," and later "the church," which in Greek means "the called out" *(ekklesia)*.

Jerusalem's officialdom was quite annoyed. They saw this preaching as heresy. They arrested two of Jesus' disciples, Peter and John,

> ### PENTECOST AND BABEL
>
> For Christians, Pentecost symbolizes God's reversal of what happened at the Tower of Babel in the Old Testament (Gen. 11:1-9). At Babel, God confused human language so that humanity would not be able to assert itself as divine. Humanity had sought there to build its own security and proclaim the glory of its own greatness. At Pentecost, God unraveled the language confusion and prepared the way for true human unity across the earth, a unity of discipleship.

and put them in prison overnight. The next day they assembled the Jerusalem Council to hear them. Peter again spoke boldly. The Council judged his words to be intolerable, but feared punishing the disciples because of their popularity with the crowds in Jerusalem. They admonished them to speak no more and let them go. But Peter replied, "Whether it is right in God's sight to listen to you rather than to God, you must judge; for we cannot keep from speaking about what we have seen and heard" (Acts 4:19-20). Thus began serious conflict between the young church and the religious and political authorities of that day, a conflict that would grow enormously.

As time passed, more and more people came to follow Jesus. Filled with the Holy Spirit, they preached powerfully. One man, Stephen, was arrested and carried before the Jerusalem Council. He went so far as to proclaim that Solomon's building of the temple in Jerusalem a thousand years before — the temple that for millennia symbolized Jewish identity — was a colossal error: "The Most High does not dwell in houses made with human hands. As the prophet says, 'Heaven is my throne and earth is my footstool. What kind of house will you build for me, says the Lord, or what is the place of my rest? Did not my hand make all these things?'" (Acts 7:48-50). Stephen then went on to declare, "You stiff-necked people, uncircumcised in heart and ears, you are forever opposing the Holy Spirit, just as your ancestors used to do" (Acts 7:51). For this speech, Stephen was stoned to death.

STONING STEPHEN

The story is told of a time when the American politician Stephen Douglas completed a particularly fiery and effective speech in his presidential debate with Abraham Lincoln. Lincoln, as he arose to reply, handed his coat to the person sitting next to him and said, "Please hold this; I'm getting ready to stone Stephen."

One of the men who oversaw Stephen's execution was Saul. A zealous young member of a Jewish religious and political movement called the Pharisees, Saul's task was to find members of this new sect called the Way and arrest them, to keep their heresy from spreading. Saul had been so successful that he had received permission from the high priest in Jerusalem to travel to Damascus (over a hundred miles to the north, in Syria) and arrest any devotees of the Way that he found there. But as he approached Damascus on his mission, "a light from heaven flashed around him. He fell to the ground and heard a voice saying to him, 'Saul, Saul, why do you persecute me?' He asked, 'Who are you, Lord?' The reply came, 'I am Jesus, whom you are persecuting. But get up and enter the city, and you will be told what you are to do'" (Acts 9:3-6). Saul went into Damascus, blind from the flash of light.

Among the followers of Christ in Damascus was a man named Ananias. God spoke to Ananias and told him to go to Saul and lay his hands on him, so that Saul might regain his sight. Ananias objected mightily, insisting that the entire event was Saul's plot to begin uncovering Christians. But God replied, "Go, for he is an instrument whom I have chosen to bring my name before Gentiles and kings and before the people of Israel" (Acts 9:15). Ananias went. He laid his hands on Saul and "something like scales fell from his eyes, and his sight was restored" (Acts 9:18). Saul was baptized, as many new followers of Christ were, and the strength of the Spirit within him increased vastly in the days ahead. Saul would be renamed Paul, and he would transform from being the leading persecutor of Christians to the leading missionary for Christ.

Meanwhile, the disciple Peter was lodging in the house of a man named Simon, a tanner in Joppa. Joppa was a seacoast town and today is next to the modern city of Tel Aviv. About noon, Peter was on Simon's roof praying. He dozed off and had a dream. As Peter was hungry, the dream was about food. He saw heaven open and something like a large sheet descend to the ground. In the sheet were all kinds of reptiles, birds, and other creatures. All of them were considered unclean in Jewish law. A voice said to Peter, "Get up, kill and eat." Peter replied, "By no means, Lord, for I have never eaten anything

THE DIGNITY OF DIFFERENCE

In his remarkable book *The Dignity of Difference,* Orthodox Jewish rabbi Jonathan Sacks says, "Every great faith has within it harsh texts which, read literally, can be taken to endorse narrow particularism, suspicion of strangers, and intolerance toward those who believe differently than we do. Every great faith also has within it sources that emphasize kinship with the stranger, empathy with the outsider, the courage that leads people to extend a hand across boundaries of estrangement or hostility. The choice is ours. Will the generous texts of our tradition serve as interpretive keys to the rest, or will the abrasive passages determine our ideas of what we are and what we are called on to do? . . . I believe that we are being summoned by God to see in the human other a trace of the divine Other, . . . to see the divine presence in the face of the stranger" (pp. 207-8).

that is profane or unclean" (Acts 10:13-15). This happened three times. (The number three, recall, denoted something heavenly.)

In Caesarea, a few miles north of Joppa, lived a man named Cornelius, a Roman centurion (or commander of one hundred soldiers), an upright, God-fearing man. Cornelius had a vision. An angel of God appeared to him and said that God was answering his prayers and his alms. The angel told Cornelius to send messengers to Joppa to bring back a man named Simon Peter. Cornelius obeyed.

While Peter was puzzling over the meaning of his dream, Cornelius's messengers arrived. They told Peter of Cornelius's visit from the angel. Peter realized that the wild animals in his vision were symbols of the Gentile world, that God was instructing him to associate with those previously considered unclean. Peter accompanied the messengers back to Caesarea. He told Cornelius the story of Jesus (Acts 10:34-43). The Holy Spirit came upon Cornelius and the others present, and Peter baptized them, proclaiming that for the first time he saw that God accepts people from any land and nation who fear God and do what is right (Acts 10:34).

This was a pivotal story in the New Testament, the clear signal that God's new kingdom was to reach into territories far beyond Israel. Up to this point, the church had been a sect within first-century Judaism. It was believed that one needed to become a Jew — that is, be circumcised (if male) and devote oneself to the law — before becoming a Christian. Now, that changed. God would work wherever God wished, whenever God wished, with whomever God wished, not being confined to Israel. Many Israelites would still hear and follow, but so would many others. In the words of Jesus' followers to whom Peter reported this episode, "God has given even to the Gentiles the repentance that leads to life" (Acts 11:18). It was a radical change, not easily accepted by the devout.

FOR DELIBERATION

1. What sort of person do you think Peter was that, on the evening of Jesus' arrest, he would deny knowing him to a slave girl (Luke 22:54-62) and then, only days later, affirm Jesus mightily in a speech before the Jerusalem Council (Acts 4:5-22)? Does that seem like pronounced spiritual vacillation to you? Does it remind you of anyone you know?

2. How do you imagine Ananias's "vision" (Acts 9:10) took place? Is there anything analogous that might happen to you? What might you do to open your eyes and ears to such a vision?

3. Describe how Ananias must have felt (Acts 9:10-19) as he made his way to welcome the great persecutor of Christians, Saul of Tarsus, into the Christian fold. Ananias could have been signing his own arrest warrant. Has God ever called upon you to do anything similarly dangerous?

4. Why would Peter, a committed disciple of Christ, fail to get the point for so long in Acts 11? Why does God have such a hard time getting through to Peter? Can you see any of yourself in him?

23

The Apostle Paul

At some point following his conversion, Saul moved to Antioch, a city far to the north of Israel, and joined the church there. The Holy Spirit spoke to the church in Antioch and told them to set aside Saul and another Christian, Barnabas, for the work God had prepared for them. After fasting and prayer, the church laid hands upon the two men and sent them off (Acts 13:1-3).

For more than a decade Saul, who by that time had taken the name Paul, engaged in missionary journeys across the eastern Mediterranean. The accounts of his missionary work begin in Acts 13 and continue to the end of the book. He took three different tours between approximately 48 and 60 C.E., visiting one city and then another, proclaiming the gospel of Jesus Christ. His normal practice was to preach, either in the local Jewish synagogue or in another public place, to assemble from those who responded a congregation of believers, to stay for a time as their teacher and guide, and then to move on to another town. He visited many of the major cities of his day: Philippi, Thessalonica, Athens, Corinth, Ephesus, Colossae, and Rome. It was primarily these sojourns that spread Christianity across the Mediterranean. Previously, the church had been a small phenomenon with a few congregations in Palestine. By the time of Paul's death it extended, in however modest numbers, over a large portion of the Greek and Roman world.

Paul's Letters

After establishing a church and moving on to another site, Paul often wrote one or more letters back to the congregation he had established. Typically, these epistles were written in response to events and issues that had been raised in the congregation, offering chastisement, encouragement, and thanksgiving as needed. The biblical books of Romans, First and Second Corinthians, Galatians, Ephesians, Philippians, Colossians, and First and Second Thessalonians are examples of these letters. Despite their modest beginnings, Paul's letters have been, for two thousand years, a primary source for Christian theology and ethics. We will look at just a few of them here.

Romans

In his letter to the church in Rome, Paul spoke of the immense and enormous love of God revealed for us, sinful humanity, in Jesus Christ, a love evidenced by the fact that it was while we were sinners, at our worst, that Christ died for us (Rom. 5:8). In words quoted repeatedly across Christian history he declared,

> I am convinced that neither death, nor life, nor angels, nor rulers, nor things present, nor things to come, nor powers, nor height, nor depth, nor anything else in all creation, will be able to separate us from the love of God in Christ Jesus our Lord. (Rom. 8:38-39)

Expressing his faith in the future God has in store both for believers and for the entire creation, Paul wrote,

> I consider that the sufferings of this present time are not worth comparing with the glory that is to be revealed to us. (Rom. 8:18)

The creation . . . has been groaning in labor pains until now; and not only the creation, but we ourselves, who have the first fruits of the Spirit, groan inwardly while we wait for adoption, the redemption of our bodies. (Rom. 8:21-23)

In light of God's love revealed for us in Jesus Christ and the hope God has promised to us and the entire creation, Paul exhorted the believers in Rome,

I appeal to you therefore, brothers and sisters, to present your bodies as a living sacrifice, holy and acceptable to God, which is your spiritual worship. Do not be conformed to this world, but be transformed by the renewing of your minds, so that you may discern what is the will of God — what is good and acceptable and perfect. (Rom. 12:1-2)

Paul wanted the church to see differently from the way the world sees, to think differently from the way the world thinks, to act differently from the way the world acts, to hope differently from the way the world hopes. It was a challenge spoken to all generations of believers.

1 Corinthians

In his letters to the church in Corinth, Paul spoke in exalted elegance of the love that originates with God.

If I speak in the tongues of mortals and of angels, but do not have love, I am a noisy gong or a clanging cymbal. If I have prophetic powers, and understand all mysteries and all knowledge, and if I have all faith, so as to remove mountains, but do not have love, I am nothing. If I give away all my possessions, and if I hand over my body so that I may boast, but do not have love, I gain nothing.

Love is patient; love is kind; love is not envious or boastful or arrogant or rude. It does not insist on its own way; it is not irritable or resentful; it does not rejoice in wrongdoing, but rejoices in the truth. It bears all things, believes all things, hopes all things, endures all things. (1 Cor. 13:1-7)

Now faith, hope, and love abide, these three; and the greatest of these is love. (1 Cor. 13:13)

Paul also spoke to the Corinthians in rich metaphor of the resurrection of the body to eternal life. Calling on the ancient jubilee image, he affirmed that the great God who sounded the trumpet every fiftieth year to release slaves from slavery, the oppressed from oppression, prisoners from prison and debtors from debt would, at a coming time, sound the cosmic trumpet to release the dead from the greatest oppression of all and give new life. It was a thrilling message!

Behold, I tell you a mystery! We shall not all sleep, but we shall all be changed, in a moment, in the twinkling of an eye, at the last trumpet. The trumpet shall sound, and the dead shall be raised imperishable, and we shall all be changed! For this perishable body must put on imperishability, and this mortal body must put on immortality. . . . Then the saying that is written will be fulfilled: Death has been swallowed up in victory! Where, O death, is your victory? Where, O death, is your sting? . . . Thanks be to God, who gives us the victory through our Lord Jesus Christ! (1 Cor. 15:51-57)

Philippians

Paul was especially fond of the church in Philippi. In his letter to them he spoke with warmth and affection about all they meant to him. And he also developed a subject of critical importance to all Christians: that is, how they were to comport themselves now that he was no longer present to lead them. How were they, new disciples of

Jesus Christ, to know how to live without their teacher? Were there rules to follow, a law to install?

Paul had once devoted himself to God's law, seeking to live every last detail. A more rigorous Pharisee there had never been:

> If anyone else has reason to be confident in the flesh, I have more: circumcised on the eighth day, a member of the people of Israel, of the tribe of Benjamin, a Hebrew born of Hebrews; as to the law, a Pharisee; as to zeal, a persecutor of the church; as to righteousness under the law, blameless. (Phil. 3:4-6)

Following God's law had been his guide and motivation.

> Yet whatever gains I had, these I have come to regard as loss because of Christ. (Phil. 3:7)

Paul had set aside a complex legal system as his guide and taken up discipleship of Jesus Christ. He now sought "the righteousness from God based on faith" (Phil. 3:9), a righteousness that came from following God's servant.

In one of the most definitive passages in the New Testament for guiding Christian behavior, Paul laid out for the Philippian church how a disciple of Christ is to decide how to live.

> Let the same mind be in you that was in Christ Jesus, who, though he was in the form of God, did not regard equality with God as something to be exploited, but emptied himself, taking the form of a slave, being born in human likeness. And being found in human form, he humbled himself and became obedient to the point of death — even death on a cross. Therefore God also highly exalted him and gave him the name that is above every name, so that at the name of Jesus every knee should bend, in heaven and on earth and under the earth, and every tongue confess that Jesus Christ is Lord, to the glory of God the Father.

> Therefore, my beloved, just as you have always obeyed me, not only in my presence, but much more in my absence, work out your own salvation with fear and trembling; for it is God who is at work in you, enabling you both to will and to work for his good pleasure. (Phil. 2:5-13)

Plug the *story* of Jesus into your mind, Paul was saying. Let the memory of Christ's oneness with God, Christ's self-emptying, Christ's becoming a human servant, Christ's obedience to death on a cross — let that memory reside firmly in your heart. Know that God established for this servant a coronation parade that began where condemned criminals reside after death — in the underworld — stretched up through earth and continued into heaven, with the knees of the faithful bowed and tongues confessing Jesus as Lord all along the way. Know that Christ resides again now with God. And know that Christ took this path for us, so that we could be one with him in his life, one with him in his death, and one with him in his resurrection. Implant that story in your mind.

And then, in awe, humility, thanksgiving, and devotion, figure out for yourselves what God's will is, what you ought to be doing in your life (as Paul put it, "work out your own salvation with fear and trembling"). If you do that, you will find God at work in your mind and heart to bring about God's good pleasure.

The Bible ends the story of Paul when he was arrested in the Jerusalem temple for "teaching everyone everywhere against our people, our law, and this place" (Acts 21:28). He was taken in chains to Rome to appeal before the emperor. He lived in Rome for two years awaiting his hearing (Acts 28:30). There is no record of what happened to him thereafter, although tradition holds that he died a martyr in Rome.

FOR DELIBERATION

1. Have you ever experienced the reality of what Paul says in Romans 8:38-39? What happened?
2. Describe the image that comes to your mind as you read aloud 1 Corinthians 15:51-57.
3. What are the primary determinants of your behavior? How much are you guided by rules? How much by stories? How much by relationships? Name some rules that affect you most. Tell a story that deeply influences you. Describe a human relationship that profoundly guides and motivates you.
4. Do you agree with Paul that Christian faith consists primarily of being guided by a story and a relationship with Christ? Or do you lean toward a strict interpretation of Jesus' words reported in Matthew, "Not one letter, not one stroke of a letter, will pass from the law until all is accomplished . . ." (Matt. 5:18)? Do you see these views as contradictory at all?

24

The Destruction of Jerusalem and the Revelation

Following the death of Israel's King Herod Agrippa in 44 C.E., tensions around Jerusalem rose to unbearable levels. Rome sent a succession of officials (called procurators) to rule and pacify the region, but each seems to have been more corrupt, more oppressive, and more contemptuous of Jewish faith than the last. Jewish extremists who preached holy war against Rome fanned the growing flames of unrest. Small bands of *sicarii*, "men of the dagger," moved about Jerusalem, kidnapping or assassinating Romans and suspected collaborators. Israel was in near revolt.

The fatal spark flared in 66 C.E., when the outrageously cruel Roman procurator, Gessius Florus, ordered a heavy tribute of gold from the treasury of the Jerusalem temple. When crowds of Jews gathered to protest, Florus turned his soldiers loose on the population. More than three thousand people were killed. The city erupted in violence. Angry Jewish rebels surged through the streets, massacring the Roman military garrison and causing Florus to flee into the countryside. The whole of Israel fell into rebel hands as the insurgence spread from town to town.

When word of the Jewish insurrection reached Rome, the Emperor Nero, not known for his moderate temperament, sent his best general, Vespasian, to clamp a lid on Israel once and for all. Vespasian moved first against towns on the Mediterranean seacoast, then into Galilee.

In the city of Gamala, east of Galilee, several thousand Jewish residents walled themselves into a mountain fortress and resisted for many days. When the Romans finally dug beneath the wall and entered the fortress, they discovered that the entire population, rather than submit to rape and massacre by the Romans, had cast themselves off a cliff into a deep river basin hundreds of feet below.

Resolutely, Vespasian moved on toward Jerusalem, taking the surrounding towns along his way. He may or may not have known that inside the walls of the holy city, various Jewish factions were fighting among themselves to see who would control the revolution. In any case, he paused in his advance when he heard that the Emperor Nero had been deposed back in Rome, and that powerful politicians wanted to make him, Vespasian, emperor. He left for Rome in 70, placing the Jerusalem siege in the capable hands of his son Titus.

Titus marched on the highly fortified city with a force of eighty thousand troops. Combining a series of fierce attacks with a military blockade that sealed the city off from its food supply, he eventually breached Jerusalem's main wall. Roman soldiers overran the city and destroyed it, pillaging and burning the temple, killing many who remained alive, and finding multitudes of others already dead. Jerusalem, the great city of God, lay in near total ruin.

Mopping up resistance across the region, the Romans turned to the Jews' final stronghold atop the 300-foot plateau of Masada overlooking the Dead Sea. At the end of three months of siege, the Romans scaled Masada, only to discover that virtually all its inhabitants — nearly a thousand men, women, and children — had committed suicide. Thus ended one of the bloodiest, cruelest, most violent eras in Israel's history. Jerusalem would be occupied by a modest number of Jews for another sixty-five years (until yet another revolt led to the final expulsion of Jews from the land in 135 C.E.), but the great city was no more than a shell of its former self.

These events are not described in the Bible. Most Jewish Christians, under great duress for their faith, had fled Jerusalem before its destruction. But the events are important to mention here both because they loom huge in Jewish history and because several New Testament writers would have had them in mind when composing their works.

The final chapter in the Bible's story appears in the Book of Revelation, or the Apocalypse. "Apocalypse," in Greek, literally means "the lifting of the veil," as a stage curtain lifts so that the audience can view events on the stage. In this book, the author sought to "lift the veil" regarding what God was doing in, through, and under severe persecution of a Christian community around 95 C.E. Believers ancient and modern have struggled to know how horrible catastrophes and persecutions can happen to faithful people, and what they mean when they do. This community of believers was no different.

The author of the Revelation called himself "John, your brother who share[s] with you in Jesus the persecution and the kingdom" (Rev. 1:9). Writing from the prison island of Patmos, the author was probably a prisoner.

The Revelation consists of seven episodes, much like seven scenes in a play, some of them long and involved, others brief. Each episode consists of seven events, four of which take place on earth (the number four signifying "earthly") and three in heaven (the number three signifying "heavenly"). Some events are cataclysmic, as with "the four horsemen of the apocalypse" who ride forth to ravage the earth (Rev. 6:1-8), and others are promissory, like the magnificent heavenly worship attended by those who "have washed their robes and made them white in the blood of the lamb" (Rev. 7:14).

Seven, we remember, was the number of completeness, finished-ness, perfected-ness. Seven times seven, or forty-nine, was the number of God's great perfection, the jubilee, the time when the trumpets of victory would blow releasing the creation from its bondage.

According to the Revelation, God's jubilee, the redemption of the entire twisted, "groaning-in-travail" world, would not happen without a monumental fight. Neither the great whore of political power nor the great beast of religious power would ever willingly relinquish their dominion! They would rage in fury at the challenge! Redemption would come only after heaven and earth were mightily shaken! This, John said, was what was happening in his time.

But God would be in the midst of the fury, directing, guiding the cataclysm toward "a new heaven and a new earth" (Rev. 21:1), toward a second creation that would be even more splendid, more "good!" than the first. In the new creation, God would dwell eternally with the faithful, wiping away "every tear from their eyes," so that "death will be no more; mourning and crying and pain will be no more" (Rev. 21:4).

The early church debated a great deal about whether the Revelation belonged in the Bible. Life is depicted there as a cosmic war between the evil and the righteous. Enemies of the righteous are despised and their bloody destruction celebrated. The earthly line between good people and evil people is starkly drawn. There is no sense that *all of us* are infected with evil, and that *all of us* need to repent and be reclaimed. There is no forgiveness of sinners. There is only final vindication of those who know they are in the right. The book does not always reflect the view of both humanity and God held across much of the rest of the Bible.

And yet the Revelation in other ways provides a fitting and compelling conclusion to the biblical story. The book affirms that life in this world is moving in a determined and specified direction set by God, even though in turmoil and conflict it is easy to lose sight of that direction. As Revelation "lifts the veil," God's dominion and purpose become clear.

Too, Revelation paints a marvelous and sparkling image of the second creation, which will be the Creator's most magnificent work (Rev. 21). All the "good!" that characterized the first creation will be even more present in the second.

Revelation also proclaims that when the final jubilee is trumpeted, a multitude of faithful "that no one could count, from every nation, from all tribes and peoples and languages," will stand before the throne of the lamb, "robed in white, with palm branches in their hands" (Rev. 7:9). The ever-expanding circle of God's redeeming love will make its way across the entire earth. The promise to Abraham that "in you all the families of the earth shall be blessed" (Gen. 12:3) will find its fulfillment.

And, finally, the Revelation brings to a magnificent conclusion the Bible's image of "the city." Throughout the Bible, the city was a troubling, ambivalent image, first appearing when Cain, recently exiled from the Garden of Eden, decided to build a new home with his own hands and by his own design (Gen. 4:17). From these beginnings, the city became a symbol of humanity's efforts to do what Cain sought to do: to reestablish his lost security in a hard and difficult world, to construct a monument to his own power, to proclaim his own glory and might. This is exactly what those who migrated into the plain of Shinar sought to build: "a city, and a tower with its top in the heavens, . . . [to] make a name for ourselves . . . [and to prevent our being] scattered abroad over the face of the whole earth" (Gen. 11:4).

In like manner the great urban centers of the ancient world — Nineveh, Babylon, Rome — lived as testimonies to the divine pretensions of their builders. They ravaged the earth with their power while pillaging and exploiting the lives of their own citizens. To the biblical writers, the city became a symbol of human arrogance, human greed, human violence, human exploitation, human effort to build security for itself.

Jerusalem, the holy city of God, was to have been different. Founded on righteousness and justice and peace, it was to have been a beacon to the nations, a light shining in darkness (Isa. 2:1-4; Micah 4:1-4). But Jerusalem turned out to be no different from the others. It repeatedly killed God's prophets and silenced the voices God sent. All human cities are finally alike, the Revelation proclaims. They ravage the earth with their power and exploit the lives of their own citizens.

And therefore the only home that will replace Eden is God's second creation, the new Jerusalem. It cannot be built; it can only be given. It will not proclaim the accomplishments of humanity, but the glory of God.

Thus, "the holy city, the new Jerusalem," descended from heaven as a bride adorned for her husband (Rev. 21:2), resplendent in its great beauty. "It has the glory of God, and a radiance like a very rare jewel, like jasper, clear as crystal" (Rev. 21:11).

And so the Revelation, and by extension the whole Bible, concludes with this message: Amid the most terrible affliction creation offers, faith provides a vision of the second creation, an image set forth to encourage the heart with hope.

FOR DELIBERATION

1. The Bible does not narrate the Roman destruction of Jerusalem, but the event cast a huge shadow across both Judaism and Christianity. It was a major factor in creating the worldview of several New Testament writers (it had not happened when Paul wrote his letters, but it had happened before at least three of the four gospels and the Revelation were written). Identify two or three events in our history that you think have most shaped your worldview and that of people around you. How have such events affected us?

2. The Revelation specializes in identifying devils and Antichrists, suggesting to some Christians in our time that we should do the same. Do you find any virtues in this pursuit? What are the dangers?

3. In Revelation, God takes strong vengeance against evil forces, torturing and then killing them. How does this compare with the picture of God in the rest of the Bible? What are the similarities and differences?

4. Revelation 20 and 21 draw a rich and compelling picture of the new creation and the holy city. Do you view it as a literal description, or more as a figurative one? What do you feel when you read these chapters?

5. How will you and I live differently in the present time if we believe that God has set the direction of life for the future time? Name specific outcomes this will create in us.

25

The Whole Story's Meaning: Psalm 90

Psalm 90 is one of the most remarkable documents in the Bible, and I find it to be a key to interpreting the whole biblical story. Its superscription reads, "A Prayer of Moses, the man of God." Out of 150 psalms, it is the only one ascribed to Moses, suggesting that it held special importance in Israel's worship. Its language suggests that it is very old, one of the earliest writings in the Bible.

The author of Psalm 90 was struggling with *the futility of human life*. He was struggling with life's brevity: we are "like grass that is renewed in the morning; in the morning it flourishes and is renewed; in the evening it fades and withers" (vv. 4-5). With life's difficulty: "The days of our life are seventy years, or perhaps eighty, if we are strong; even then their span is only toil and trouble; they are soon gone, and we fly away" (v. 10). With life's pain: "All our days pass away under your wrath" (v. 9); "your wrath is as great as the fear that is due you" (v. 11). This psalmist knew how barren human years can be, how seemingly pointless. Countless individuals have wrestled with this sense of futility throughout history; to give one famous example, recall Shakespeare's famous lines from *Macbeth*:

> To-morrow, and to-morrow, and to-morrow,
> Creeps in this petty pace from day to day

To the last syllable of recorded time,
And all our yesterdays have lighted fools
The way to dusty death. Out, out, brief candle!
Life's but a walking shadow, a poor player
That struts and frets his hour upon the stage
And then is heard no more: It is a tale
Told by an idiot, full of sound and fury,
Signifying nothing.

But the psalmist addressed this futility by setting our few years in the context of God's eternity. "Before the mountains were brought forth, or ever you had formed the earth and the world, from everlasting to everlasting you are God" (v. 2). "A thousand years in your sight are as yesterday when it is past, like a watch in the night" (v. 4). God is "from everlasting to everlasting," as eternal as we are brief, as enormous as we are tiny, as rich in meaning as we are pointless.

It is in relation to the "from everlasting to everlasting" one that we find our "dwelling place" (v. 1), our home, our identity. Our short and struggling lives do not uncover their significance within their own boundaries. They find it only in relation to God's eternity, to the great expanse that invisibly surrounds us.

Therefore, the psalmist prays fervently to God: "So teach us to count our days that we may gain a wise heart" (v. 12). Show us from your eternity how to live our brevity. Enlighten our small hearts with your vast wisdom.

Psalm 90 replies to life's futility with a prayer rooted deep within the psalmist's faith.

The Bible, I believe, is Psalm 90 writ large. We find in its pages all the wiles and machinations of the human heart, the intrigues, the plots, the greeds, the lusts, the exploitations, the savageries. We find earthquakes and droughts, famines and floods, storms at sea, fevers and lame legs, blind eyes, withered hands and sick children. We find war and violence, pride and arrogance, humiliation and defeat, momentary success and profound failure, hope and disillusionment — everything that happens in our world.

And the question raised by these sordid, seemingly pointless events is: does anything matter? Win some, lose some, enjoy some, suffer some, live some, die some — is there finally any consequence? Does it all signify anything? In the words of another biblical writer, "What do people gain from all the toil at which they toil under the sun? . . . I saw all the deeds that are done under the sun; and see, all is vanity and a chasing after wind" (Eccles. 1:3, 14).

To this futility the Bible speaks. Surrounding our short lives is an everlasting to everlasting that offers intense meaning. Transcending our tiny, limited vision is a vastly greater wisdom. God stoops to us, relates to us, listens to us, communes with is, sharing a wisdom that is far above our wisdom and ways that are infinitely beyond our ways.

And what wisdom does God impart? It is conveyed through several key concepts prominent in the biblical story.

God's wisdom teaches *justice* (*mishpat* in Hebrew), what God demonstrated with Israel in Egypt. Justice involves hearing the cries, perceiving the plight of the lowliest, and casting one's influence for their good. It involves letting the prayers of the overlooked make their way into the ears of those with strength. Justice means elevating to vital significance the interests of the poor, the widow, the orphan, and the slave, when the pressures of big-ticket influence are pressing hard to squeeze them out. It means taking empathetic notice of the families that live in public housing projects, of the women who make our motel room beds, of the men who nail on our roof shingles, of the workers who clean up our offices at night, of the garbage crews who haul away our trash, of the clerks who stock our grocery shelves, realizing that these, too, have people they love, food they must buy, rent they must pay, education they must provide, and medical care they need. Justice means tilting one's attention, and the laws and practices of one's society, toward those whom Jesus called "the least of these my brothers and sisters" (Matt. 25:40).

God's wisdom teaches *righteousness (tzedakah)*. Righteousness is what God exhibited in creating a covenant community. It means living a good and upright life among one's people, a life of integrity, of guiding values and worthwhile pursuits. Righteousness means working to build hospitals and schools and retirement homes and synagogues and churches to support the common good. Righteousness means having in one's heart the conviction that we are all in it together, that the whole community's benefit is a primary purpose in my life.

God's wisdom teaches *faithfulness (emunah)*. Faithfulness is what God showed in making promises to Abraham and keeping them through the generations. It is God's traveling ahead of Israel in the Sinai Desert to locate water holes where the people could drink (Exod. 15:22–17:7). It is God's calling on Rahab to help Israel spy out the Promised Land (Josh. 2). Faithfulness is God's appointing Cyrus the Persian to return Israel home after forty years of Babylonian exile (Isa. 40). Faithfulness is God's sending Jesus, the Messiah, to fulfill the vows of more than a millennium before (Matt. 1, Luke 2). Faithfulness is Jesus' commitment, "Remember, I am with you always, to the end of the age" (Matt. 28:20). When I was twelve years old, I was in my father's downtown office late one afternoon, waiting for a ride home. A work colleague came in and asked my father, "Owen, did you get Bill Harmon's signature?" My father replied, "With Bill Harmon, you don't need his signature; all you need is his word." I have thought to myself many times, "What a great reputation to have!" Therein is faithfulness: dependably saying what you will do, and doing what you have said.

God's wisdom teaches *love (hesed)*. Love is what God embodied in Jesus, who, in Paul's words, "though he was in the form of God, did not count his equality with God a thing to be clutched, but emptied himself, taking the form of a servant," showing us the way, the truth, and the life (Phil. 2:6-7). Love is caring seriously about someone besides yourself, giving your life for those among whom you dwell.

And, beneath it all, God teaches *discipleship*. God sent Jesus to make disciples — first twelve, then the whole world.

Discipleship means being present when he heals lepers and cures the fevers of everyday people. Watching in awe as he stills a storm on the Sea of Galilee (Mark 4:35-41). Serving as he feeds five thousand with five loaves and two fish, and being amazed when we take up more scraps than we served to begin with (Mark 6:30-44).

Discipleship means hearing him say, "You are the salt of the earth" (Matt. 5:13), and realizing that he is appointing us to inject special savor and taste into mundane life. It means receiving his words, "Blessed are the pure in heart" (Matt. 5:8), and knowing that he is calling us not to participate in the world's deceit and guile.

Discipleship means being present when he speaks with the woman at the well, and watching him redeem her life (John 8:1-11). It means being surprised when an impertinent woman barges into an all-male meal to anoint him with costly oil, and watching him honor her for knowing the importance of the moment (Mark 14:3-9). It means hearing him say, "Inasmuch as you have done it unto one of the least of these my brothers and sisters, you have done it unto me" (Matt. 25:40), and sensing that those words are to guide us when he is no longer present.

Discipleship means being with him in the garden when he prays, and watching his sweat become like great drops of blood falling to the ground (Mark 14:32-42). It means being present when soldiers arrest him (Mark 14:43-50), hearing the crowd shout, "Crucify him! Crucify him!" (Mark 15:6-15), seeing his cross on the hillside, and then, three days later, viewing his tomb empty (Mark 16). It means being together in a locked building when suddenly he is with us, saying, "Peace be with you" (Luke 24:36).

Discipleship means experiencing his Spirit breaking out among us, empowering us to speak boldly in the marketplaces (Acts 2). It means becoming the first church, those called to live as his followers. It means confessing how he, in a self-centered and self-aggrandizing world, came not to be served but to serve, and to give his life as a ransom for many.

Devoting ourselves to justice, to righteousness, to faithfulness, to love, to discipleship: this is what will cause our short stay on this planet to find eternal meaning, and it will establish the from-everlasting-to-everlasting one as our dwelling place through all ages.

For Deliberation

1. When have you been most aware of the brevity of human life? When have "seventy years, or perhaps eighty" seemed most like "a watch in the night" — that is, a very short time?

2. When has life seemed the most futile to you? When has our span of years seemed most like "toil and trouble" after which "we are soon gone and we fly away"?

3. What do you make of Psalm 90's implication that the full meaning of a human life can come only from "the everlasting to everlasting" rather than from within the life itself? Do we need God to give our lives meaning? Why or why not?

4. What are the sources of the greatest meaning in your life? Do they have to do with justice, righteousness, faithfulness, love, discipleship?

26

One Story: God's Call

We began this book with two assertions: that the Bible, despite its enormous diversity, tells one story that has a clear and compelling meaning; and that, through the Bible's story, God issues a call we cannot ignore. Now that we have heard the story, let us close by expanding on those two assertions.

The Bible is one story of God's creativity: of the first creation which is past, and the second creation which is to come.

The Bible is one story of the faithful, devoted, caring, self-giving people we can be. It is also one story of humanity's obstinate heart, of our unending insistence on doing things our way in pursuit of our purposes.

The Bible is one story of God's commitment to relate to us: not just to kings and rulers, but to common people; not just in prosperity, but through the valley of the shadow of death; not just when we know God is present, but when we suspect God has abandoned us.

The Bible is one story of God's amazing love, a love that tracks us even into the most remote places of our waywardness.

The Bible is one story of God's self-giving, through words and mighty acts, in flesh that dwelled among us full of grace and truth, in the Spirit that Jesus promised to his followers.

The Bible is one story of God's amazing power to raise death to life, to start with what is hopeless and bring about amazing outcomes.

The Bible is one story of God's intention to restore peace in the human family, a family rent by the violence of Cain against his brother, by the vengeance of Lamech against his offender, by the aggression that easily rises in the human heart. Through all this violence, God promises: "The wolf shall dwell with the lamb, and the leopard shall lie down with the kid . . . (Isa. 11:6). "[God] will wipe away every tear from their eyes. Death will be no more" (Rev. 21:4). "Peace I leave with you; my peace I give to you. I do not give to you as the world gives. Do not let your hearts be troubled, and do not let them be afraid" (John 14:27). And God challenges, "Blessed are the peacemakers, for they will be called children of God" (Matt. 5:9).

Through its huge diversity of writers, of ideas, of beliefs, of claims, the Bible is a singular witness to this one story. And throughout the Bible, God called people.

God called Abraham and Sarah to leave their home, their family, their security, and to migrate into a country they did not know.

God called Moses to present himself before Pharaoh and lead Israel out of Egypt.

God called Samuel to become a prophet, to anoint Israel's first kings, Saul and David.

God called Ruth, a foreigner from Moab, to exemplify faithfulness and ultimately to be a forebear of Jesus Christ.

God called Isaiah to speak to a people who would not hear, whose eyes were blind and whose ears were sealed.

God called Mary, a poor young woman, to give birth to God incarnate.

God called four fishermen, a tax collector, a zealot, a bookkeeper, to become Christ's disciples.

God called a zealous Pharisee, Paul, to take on a new heart and become Christ's missionary to the world.

Throughout the Bible, God called people. And God calls us too. Calls us to leave the accustomed and travel into the unfamiliar. Calls us to speak words of promise and hope, but also words of challenge and admonishment. Calls us to do things we had not previously planned and for which we were not prepared. Calls us to risk our lives for whatever God has in mind.

This, I believe, is the primary thing that happens in the Bible: God calls *us*.

"The Son of Man came not to be served but to serve, and to give his life as a ransom for many" (Mark 10:45) — that is God's call to us.

"Blessed are the pure in heart, for they will see God" (Matt. 5:8) — that is God's call to us.

"The spirit of the Lord is upon me, because he has anointed me to bring good news to the poor" (Luke 4:18) — that is God's call to us.

"Do not be conformed to this world, but be transformed by the renewing of your minds, so that you may discern what is the will of God — what is good and acceptable and perfect" (Rom. 12:2) — that is God's call to us.

"Go . . . and make disciples of all nations, baptizing them in the name of the Father and of the Son and of the Holy Spirit, and teaching them to obey everything I have commanded you" (Matt. 28:19-20) — that is God's call to us.

"Let justice roll down like waters, and righteousness like an everflowing stream" (Amos 5:24) — that is God's call to us.

We register all the normal objections, the same objections Moses voiced when God called him to lead Israel out of Egypt. "Who am I, God; you can certainly find someone better than me." "Who are you, God; I'm not very religious, and I don't know you that well." "They will scoff at me, God, and reject the idea that I have heard a god call!" "I am not prepared to do what you want done, God; it's not my talent."

In response to our objections, God speaks a simple word: "Go!" We cannot walk away unaffected.

A young woman who recently graduated from college is spending three years working for an anti-hunger network in Bolivia.

The senior partner in a law firm is so moved by the plight of three eight-year-old boys that he devotes the next half-decade of his life to building a community center next to the public housing project where they live.

A retired couple travels every week to a distant part of their town to read library books with children in the lowest-scoring elementary school in their city.

A woman becomes so caught up in the plight of a ten-month-old girl in a Guatemala City barrio that she returns home to establish the second largest refugee resettlement agency in her state.

A woman spends a portion of every day visiting infirm, home-bound members of her church, letting them know that they are cared for and that their lives are deeply significant.

Our world has a vast overabundance of self-centeredness, self-occupation, self-indulgence, self-serving. The Bible calls us to a larger vision — to see a world bigger than the space close around us. To see a family larger than our immediate relatives and friends. To see importance beyond our normal daily attention. To see a God who transcends the gods we fashion to serve our little worlds. The Bible calls us outside ourselves, to live in a greater space, a larger family, a fuller universe, with a God who is always bigger than we think.

God calls us! And God awaits our answer. Will we, with faithful people across the Bible, reply "Here am I, Lord, send me"?

For Deliberation

1. We began this study with the assertion that there is one God and one us, the same two subjects acting throughout the Bible (and into today). List, now, major things we have learned about God. What are God's most significant characteristics? In looking over the whole of the biblical story, do you see things about God that you didn't notice before?

2. Now list major things we have learned about us, about humanity. What sort of people are we? What are our greatest strengths and weaknesses? What do you imagine it must be like for God to want to associate with us?

3. Name something to which God has called you at some time past.

How did that call come? Did the Bible play a role? How did you respond? What call do you hear God speaking to you today?

4. In one of the best sermons I have ever heard, the preacher, preaching on "How Faith Grows," said, "Faith grows by risk, by associating ourselves with situations of human need in which we cannot survive without God's help, and then watching what happens." Does your experience say that faith grows by risk? What risks have you taken on behalf of people who need you? What has happened?

Chronology of the Bible's Story

Note that many dates are approximate.

Creation, Garden of Eden, Noah, Tower of Babel	prehistory
The Patriarchs: Abraham, Isaac, Jacob, and Joseph	between 2000 and 1300 B.C.E.
Moses	possibly 1275-1200 B.C.E.
The Exodus	possibly around 1250 B.C.E.
Trek through the Sinai wilderness	possibly 1250-1200 B.C.E.
Entry into the Promised Land	possibly around 1200 B.C.E.
Conquest and period of the judges	possibly 1200-1020 B.C.E.
First king of Israel: Saul	approximately 1020-1000 B.C.E.
Israel's great king, David (prophet Nathan)	1000-961 B.C.E.
King Solomon	961-922 B.C.E.
Split of the nation: Israel (north) and Judah (south)	922 B.C.E.
Era of the nation Israel (prophets Elijah, Elisha, Amos)	922-721 B.C.E.

Fall of Israel to the Assyrians	721 B.C.E.
Era of the nation Judah (prophets Micah, Isaiah, Jeremiah, Ezekiel)	922-587 B.C.E.
Fall of Judah to the Babylonians	587 B.C.E.
Babylonian exile	587-539 B.C.E.
Return from exile (prophet Second Isaiah, chapters 40–66 of the Book of Isaiah)	539-520 B.C.E.
Persian rule (Ezra, Nehemiah)	539-332 B.C.E.
Greek rule (Judas Maccabeus)	332-63 B.C.E.
Roman rule	63 B.C.E. through New Testament period
Reign of Herod the Great	39-4 B.C.E.
Birth of Jesus	probably 4 B.C.E.
Crucifixion of Jesus	probably 29 C.E.
Saul's conversion on the Damascus Road	around 34-44 C.E.
Paul's missionary journeys and letters	around 47-63 C.E.
Gospel of Mark written	decade of the 60s C.E.
Destruction of Jerusalem by Rome	70 C.E.
Gospels of Matthew and Luke written	probably 70-90 C.E.
Gospel of John and the Revelation written	decade of the 90s C.E.

Daily Bible Readings

I, the author, recommend that study groups consider the twenty-six chapters in this book over the fifty-two weeks of a year, one chapter every two weeks. With that in mind, I have prepared daily Bible readings to support the study over a one-year period. If you choose to study through the book in six months or nine months or two years, you can adjust the readings accordingly. The purpose of the readings is to engage you with texts that have created what you are studying. I suggest you view them in two ways, not omitting either. First, treat them as historical texts that form the Bible's story, original documents that contribute to our knowledge and comprehension. Second, treat them as holy writings, Scripture, texts through which God speaks to us and lays claim on us. I suggest that with each text, you add thoughtful meditation and prayer, a prayer for open ears and heart to hear what God is saying, and that you ponder seriously the meaning of the text in your own life.

Chapter 1: Introduction

DAY 1	Psalm 23	*There is no text in Scripture more treasured by believers.*
DAY 2	John 3:16-21	*Christians everywhere recite John 3:16.*
DAY 3	1 Cor. 13	*At whose wedding has this text not been read?*
DAY 4	Jer. 20:7-18	*Jeremiah lamented mightily over Israel's waywardness.*
DAY 5	Acts 10:34-43	*Luke exhilarated that God was enlarging the church beyond Israel.*
DAY 6	1 Thess. 4:13-18	*This text has been the basis for modern day "left behind" theology, the belief that in "the Rapture" good people will be taken up to enjoy all the blessings of heaven while evil people are sent to eternal punishment in the torments of hell.*
DAY 7	Matt. 5:1-12	*God calls believers to love and peace.*
DAY 8	Matt. 5:21-26	*God calls believers to forgiveness and reconciliation.*
DAY 9	Rev. 19:17-21	*The beast and all who worship him are burnt in the lake of fire.*
DAY 10	Psalm 65	*A farmer's prayer of thanks: one of the many types of biblical literature.*
DAY 11	Luke 15:3-10	*Luke paints two pictures of God, as shepherd and housewife.*
DAY 12	Deut. 21:18-21	*Does this not seem horribly vindictive to us?*
DAY 13	Luke 15:11-32	*Luke paints another picture of God, as a forgiving father.*
DAY 14	Luke 4:1-15	*Jesus and Satan both argue by quoting biblical texts.*

Chapter 2: Contours of the Land

DAY 1	1 Sam. 3	*All Israel, from Dan to Beersheba, saw that Samuel was a prophet.*
DAY 2	Hosea 1:1-9	*God vowed through Hosea to slay Israel in the valley of Jezreel.*
DAY 3	1 Kings 1:32-40	*Solomon, King David's son, is anointed king in the waters of the Spring of Gihon.*
DAY 4	1 Kings 32:27-31	*King Hezekiah dug an underground tunnel to carry water from the Spring of Gihon inside the*

		Jerusalem walls; Hezekiah's tunnel is still in place to this day.
DAY 5	**1 Kings 17:1-16**	*Terrible drought descended upon Israel.*
DAY 6	**Gen. 2:4-9**	*God started creation with a dry desert, parched, lifeless dirt, and brought forth a stream of water to give it life.*
DAY 7	**Gen. 2:10-14**	*God provided more-than-abundant water in the Garden of Eden, a great blessing for humanity.*
DAY 6	**Gen. 12:10-20**	*Because of drought, Abraham and family traveled into Egypt seeking food.*
DAY 8	**Exod. 17:1-7**	*Israel thirsted greatly on their trek through the Sinai Desert.*
DAY 9	**Luke 16:19-31**	*Luke pictured Hades as a place with no water!*
DAY 10	**Isa. 35**	*Isaiah prophesied that parched desert lands would blossom into a garden.*
DAY 11	**Isa. 55:1-3**	*God prepared a great feast of water and food for Israel on their return from the Babylonian exile.*
DAY 12	**John 7:37-39**	*Jesus offered "a river of living water."*
DAY 13	**Isa. 19:23-25**	*Isaiah looked forward to the day when God would build a highway of reconciliation between the two great warring powers of his world, Egypt and Assyria, and would turn their hearts to peace.*
DAY 14	**Rev. 22:1-5**	*God will place a "river of the water of life" in the second creation.*

Chapter 3: Contours of the Mind

DAY 1	**Gen. 1:1-5**	*God began creation with a "deep," a chaotic mass of dark water, and a wind from God swept over the face of the deep. Creation started with the taming of this watery mass.*
DAY 2	**Psalm 74:12-17**	*Another version of creation: God conquered dragons of the sea and deep water monsters.*
DAY 3	**Gen. 7**	*Humankind was so evil that God sent a flood to erase the creation and start over.*
DAY 4	**Exod. 14:21-31**	*God gave birth to Israel by commanding the waters of the Red Sea to part so that Israel could escape Egypt.*
DAY 5	**Jonah 2**	*From deep beneath the waters of the sea, Jonah called for God's help.*

DAY 6	Psalm 107:1-3, 23-32	*God saved people in terrible trouble on the great waters.*
DAY 7	Mark 4:35-41	*Jesus stilled a storm on the waters.*
DAY 8	Rev. 21:1-4	*In God's second creation, there will be no more sea, according to John!*
DAY 9	Exod. 16:4-8	*In the barren desert, God provided food.*
DAY 10	Mark 6:30-44	*To a hungry multitude, God provided food.*
DAY 11	John 6:35-40	*Jesus is the bread of life.*
DAY 12	Matt. 6:7-15	*Jesus taught us to pray for daily bread.*
DAY 13	Isa. 40:12-31	*A great testimony to the oneness of God.*
DAY 14	Psalm 103:15-18	*The Bible's most oft-used characterization of the human plight: we are like grass that blossoms gloriously but quickly fades.*

Chapter 4: The Beginning: Good!

DAY 1	Gen. 1:1-19	*Four days of creation.*
DAY 2	Gen. 1:20–2:3	*God created living beings and rested.*
DAY 3	Gen. 2:4b-17	*God created a man and provided for him.*
DAY 4	Gen. 2:18-25	*God created birds, animals, and then woman.*
DAY 5	Psalm 8	*God made humans just "a little lower than God."*
DAY 6	Psalm 19	*The creation declares God's glory.*
DAY 7	Psalm 24	*The earth is the LORD's.*
DAY 8	Psalm 29	*The LORD rules the creation!*
DAY 9	Psalm 33	*The earth is full of God's steadfast love.*
DAY 10	Psalm 46	*The mountains shake and the waters roar.*
DAY 11	Psalm 98	*The whole of creation acclaims God!*
DAY 12	Psalm 104	*God, the great Creator!*
DAY 13	Psalm 145	*"His compassion is over all that he has made."*
DAY 14	Psalm 148	*Let the whole creation praise God!*

Chapter 5: Not So Good

DAY 1	Gen. 3:1-12	*Adam blames Eve; Eve blames the snake.*
DAY 2	Gen. 3:13-19	*God issues great curse.*
DAY 3	Gen. 3:20-21	*God issues sustaining grace.*
DAY 4	Gen. 3:22-24	*Eviction from the Garden.*

DAY 5	Gen. 4:1-16	*Murder enters human life.*
DAY 6	Gen. 4:17-24	*And then vengeance murder.*
DAY 7	Gen. 4:25-26	*The birth of Seth.*
DAY 8	Gen. 5	*The ancestors.*
DAY 9	Gen. 6:1-8	*The wickedness of humanity.*
DAY 10	Gen. 6:9-22	*God called Noah.*
DAY 11	Gen. 7	*The great flood.*
DAY 12	Gen. 8:1-19	*The waters subsided.*
DAY 13	Gen. 9:1-17	*God's covenant with Noah.*
DAY 14	Gen. 11:1-9	*The tower of Babel.*

Chapter 6: The Patriarchs

DAY 1	Gen. 12:1-4a	*God called Abram.*
DAY 2	Gen. 15	*God made a covenant with Abram.*
DAY 3	Gen. 18:1-15	*Three messengers brought a word from God to Abram and Sarai.*
DAY 4	Gen. 21:1-7	*Isaac was born.*
DAY 5	Gen. 21:1-14	*God tested Abram.*
DAY 6	Gen. 24	*Isaac married Rebekah.*
DAY 7	Gen. 25:19-28	*Esau and Jacob, twins, struggled to be the firstborn.*
DAY 8	Gen. 25:29-34	*Esau sold his birthright to the scheming Jacob.*
DAY 9	Gen. 27	*Jacob tricked Esau out of their father's blessing.*
DAY 10	Gen. 28:10-22	*Jacob had a dream at Bethel.*
DAY 11	Gen. 29:15-30	*Uncle Laban turned out to be even more devious than Jacob.*
DAY 12	Gen. 32:22-32	*Jacob wrestled with God at Peniel.*
DAY 13	Gen. 38	*Tamar confronted Judah.*
DAY 14	Gen. 50:15-21	*Joseph forgave his brothers.*

Chapter 7: Exodus and Wilderness

DAY 1	Exod. 1:8-22	*Israel was oppressed in Egypt.*
DAY 2	Exod. 2:1-10	*Moses was born and hidden in the reeds.*
DAY 3	Exod. 2:11-22	*Moses killed an Egyptian and became a fugitive.*
DAY 4	Exod. 3:1-12	*God called Moses.*

DAY 5	Exod. 7:14-25	*God sent the first plague on Egypt: water turned to blood.*
DAY 6	Exod. 12:21-32	*God sent the tenth plague: the death of Egypt's firstborn.*
DAY 7	Exod. 14	*Israel passed through the waters of the Red Sea.*
DAY 8	Exod. 16	*Israel complained against God, and God sent manna.*
DAY 9	Exod. 19	*God consecrated Israel.*
DAY 10	Exod. 20:1-21	*God gave Israel the Ten Commandments.*
DAY 11	Exod. 32–34	*Israel made for themselves golden calves to worship, and God grew exceedingly angry.*
DAY 12	Exod. 40	*The tabernacle was erected, and the glory of God inhabited it.*
DAY 13	Lev. 25:8-56	*God instituted the year of Jubilee.*
DAY 14	Num. 9:15-23	*The cloud by day and the pillar of fire by night: God led Israel through the wilderness of Sinai.*

Chapter 8: The Promised Land

DAY 1	Deut. 4:1-14	*Moses addressed Israel before they entered the Promised Land.*
DAY 2	Deut. 6:1-9	*God gave the great commandment.*
DAY 3	Deut. 8	*God promised great prosperity but sternly warned against haughtiness.*
DAY 4	Deut. 15:7-11	*God commanded generosity toward the needy.*
DAY 5	Deut. 17:14-20	*God stipulated how the king was to act.*
DAY 6	Deut. 30:11-20	*Israel was to obey God's law.*
DAY 7	Deut. 34	*Moses died, and Joshua was appointed in his place.*
DAY 8	Josh. 1:1-9	*God commissioned Joshua.*
DAY 9	Josh. 2	*God claimed Rahab.*
DAY 10	Josh. 3	*Israel crossed the Jordan River and entered the Promised Land.*
DAY 11	Josh. 4	*Israel set memorial rocks at the place of their crossing.*
DAY 12	Josh. 6	*Israel defeated and destroyed Jericho.*
DAY 13	Josh. 8:1-29	*Ai was captured and destroyed.*
DAY 14	Josh. 13:15-32	*God distributed the Promised Land among Israel's tribes, giving each an "inheritance."*

Chapter 9: Era of the Judges

DAY 1	Josh. 24:1-15	*God renewed the covenant with Israel.*
DAY 2	Judg. 3:7-30	*Othniel and Ehud led Israel.*
DAY 3	Judg. 4	*Deborah and Barak led Israel.*
DAY 4	Judg. 5	*The song of Deborah and Barak.*
DAY 5	Judg. 6	*God called a very reluctant Gideon.*
DAY 6	Judg. 7	*By fear and terror, Gideon defeated the Midianites.*
DAY 7	Judg. 11	*Jephthah defeated the Ammonites and sacrificed his daughter.*
DAY 8	Judg. 13	*Samson was born.*
DAY 9	Judg. 14	*Samson married.*
DAY 10	Judg. 15	*Samson defeated the Philistines.*
DAY 11	Judg. 16:1-22	*Samson loved Delilah.*
DAY 12	Judg. 16:23-31	*Samson died, along with the lords of the Philistines.*
DAY 13	Ruth 1–2	*Naomi, Ruth, and Boaz.*
DAY 14	Ruth 3–4	*Ruth married Boaz.*

Chapter 10: The United Monarchy

DAY 1	1 Sam. 4	*Israel battled the Philistines, unsuccessfully.*
DAY 2	1 Sam. 5	*The ark of the covenant was captured.*
DAY 3	1 Sam. 6	*The ark was returned and placed at Kiriath-jearim.*
DAY 4	1 Sam. 8	*Israel demanded a king to lead them, but there was also dissent!*
DAY 5	1 Sam. 9:1-26	*Saul was chosen as king.*
DAY 6	1 Sam. 17	*David defeated Goliath.*
DAY 7	2 Sam. 5	*David was anointed king of all Israel, and defeated the Philistines.*
DAY 8	2 Sam. 7:1-17	*God made a covenant with David through the prophet Nathan.*
DAY 9	2 Sam. 8	*David was an exceedingly successful military leader.*
DAY 10	2 Sam. 11	*David committed adultery with Bathsheba.*
DAY 11	2 Sam. 12:1-23	*Nathan condemned David and the child died.*
DAY 12	1 Kings 3	*Solomon's wisdom.*
DAY 13	1 Kings 6:1-22	*Solomon built the Jerusalem temple dedicated to God.*
DAY 14	1 Kings 1:1-13	*Solomon caused rebellion in his own kingdom.*

Chapter 11: The Beginning of the Divided Monarchy

DAY 1	1 Kings 12:1-19	*The northern tribes seceded.*
DAY 2	1 Kings 16:29–17:7	*The prophet Elijah declared drought on the land for King Ahab's apostasy.*
DAY 3	1 Kings 17:8-24	*Elijah stayed with the widow of Zarephath.*
DAY 4	1 Kings 18:1-19	*Elijah encountered King Ahab.*
DAY 5	1 Kings 18:20-40	*Elijah contested with the priests of Baal.*
DAY 6	1 Kings 18:41-46	*The drought ended.*
DAY 7	1 Kings 19:1-10	*Elijah fled Jezebel.*
DAY 8	1 Kings 19:11-18	*Elijah encountered God at Mt. Horeb.*
DAY 9	1 Kings 21:1-16	*Jezebel seized Naboth's property in Jezreel.*
DAY 10	1 Kings 21:17-28	*Elijah pronounced God's sentence upon Ahab and Jezebel.*
DAY 11	1 Kings 22:1-40	*Ahab was defeated and died.*
DAY 12	2 Kings 2:13-25	*Elisha succeeded Elijah and performed wonders.*
DAY 13	2 Kings 4:8-37	*Elisha raised a child from death.*
DAY 14	2 Kings 5:1-19	*Elisha healed Naaman the Syrian.*

Chapter 12: Great Struggle and Great Hope

DAY 1	Amos 2:6-16	*Amos declared God's judgment on Israel.*
DAY 2	Amos 4:1-3	*Amos prophesied against the elegant women of Bashan.*
DAY 3	Amos 5:1-13	*Amos predicted Israel's ruin.*
DAY 4	Amos 5:16-24	*Let justice roll down like waters.*
DAY 5	Amos 6:1-7	*Amos decried the wealthy who ignored the poor.*
DAY 6	Amos 7:10-17	*Amos spoke to the priest Amaziah.*
DAY 7	Amos 9:11-15	*Amos spoke God's promise.*
DAY 8	Isa. 6	*God called Isaiah to be a prophet.*
DAY 9	Isa. 2:1-4	*Isaiah prophesied that God would beat swords into plowshares.*
DAY 10	Isa. 5:8-30	*Isaiah spoke God's judgment on Israel.*
DAY 11	Isa. 9:2b-7	*Unto us a child is born.*
DAY 12	Isa. 11:6-9	*The wolf shall dwell with the lamb.*
DAY 13	Isa. 19:23-25	*God will build a highway connecting monumental adversaries.*
DAY 14	Isa. 35	*The desert will blossom!*

Chapter 13: Reform, Destruction, and Exile

DAY 1	**2 Kings 22–23:25**	*King Josiah instituted drastic reform.*
DAY 2	**Jer. 1**	*God called Jeremiah.*
DAY 3	**Jer. 5:1-11**	*Jeremiah declared Jerusalem faithless.*
DAY 4	**Jer. 6:1-8**	*"The doom is imminent!" declared Jeremiah.*
DAY 5	**Jer. 7:1-15**	*Jeremiah's sermon in Jerusalem.*
DAY 6	**2 Kings 25**	*Babylon destroyed Jerusalem.*
DAY 7	**Psalm 137**	*Israel's fierce anger at Babylon.*
DAY 8	**Ezek. 1**	*God sent a vision to Ezekiel: a wheeled vehicle.*
DAY 9	**Ezek. 2:1–3:11**	*Ezekiel's vision of the scroll.*
DAY 10	**Ezek. 3:12-21**	*Ezekiel in exile by the River Chebar.*
DAY 11	**Ezek. 15**	*The useless vine.*
DAY 12	**Ezek. 20:33-44**	*God will restore Israel.*
DAY 13	**Ezek. 37:1-14**	*Dry bones lived!*
DAY 14	**Jer. 31:31-34**	*God will write the covenant upon Israel's heart.*

Chapter 14: Return

DAY 1	**Ezra 1**	*King Cyrus of Persia ended Israel's captivity in Babylon.*
DAY 2	**Isa. 40:1-11**	*A triumphant parade through the desert that will crown God king.*
DAY 3	**Isa. 40:27-31**	*They shall rise up with wings like eagles.*
DAY 4	**Isa. 42:1-9**	*God has called a servant.*
DAY 5	**Isa. 49:1-6**	*A light to the nations.*
DAY 6	**Isa. 51**	*The Lord will comfort Israel.*
DAY 7	**Isa. 52:13–53:12**	*The suffering servant of the Lord.*
DAY 8	**Isa. 54**	*God will make an eternal covenant of peace.*
DAY 9	**Isa. 55:1-6**	*God's great banquet.*
DAY 10	**Isa. 55:6-11**	*God's ways higher than our ways.*
DAY 11	**Isa. 58:6-14**	*The covenant God establishes.*
DAY 12	**Isa. 60:1-18**	*The ingathering.*
DAY 13	**Isa. 61**	*God's jubilee.*
DAY 14	**Isa. 65:17-25**	*The new creation.*

Chapter 15: Reconstitution and Beyond

DAY 1	Neh. 1	Nehemiah was greatly troubled over the plight of Jerusalem.
DAY 2	Neh. 2	Nehemiah and the town officials decided to rebuild the walls.
DAY 3	Neh. 4	A hostile plot against building the walls was thwarted.
DAY 4	Neh. 5:1-13	Nehemiah stopped the oppression of the powerless.
DAY 5	Neh. 5:14-19	Nehemiah asked God to remember his goodwill.
DAY 6	Neh. 6:1-14	Wiles of the enemies were foiled.
DAY 7	Neh. 6:15–7:4	The wall was completed and guards set in place.
DAY 8	Ezra 3:1-7	Worship in Jerusalem was resumed.
DAY 9	Ezra 3:8–4:24	Temple foundations were laid, but then great opposition.
DAY 10	Ezra 6	King Darius of Persia issued a proclamation, and the temple was completed.
DAY 11	Ezra 7	King Artaxerxes wrote a letter of decree to Ezra.
DAY 12	Ezra 9:5–10:5	Ezra prayed mightily to God, and the people responded.
DAY 13	Psalm 100	Make a joyful noise before the Lord!
DAY 14	Psalm 136	God's steadfast love endures forever.

Chapter 16: King of the Jews

DAY 1	Matt. 1:18–2:12	Jesus was born in Bethlehem.
DAY 2	Matt. 2:13-23	Herod sought to kill the newborn king.
DAY 3	Luke 2:1-20	Angels marked his birth and shepherds gathered.
DAY 4	Luke 2:22-52	Jesus was presented in the Jerusalem temple.
DAY 5	John 1:1-18	The Word became flesh and dwelt among us, full of grace and truth.
DAY 6	Luke 4:16-30	Jesus preached in Nazareth.
DAY 7	Luke 5:1-11	Jesus called disciples.
DAY 8	Luke 5:17-26	Jesus debated the Pharisees, highly devout religious people.
DAY 9	Mark 4:35-41	Jesus stilled a storm on the sea.
DAY 10	Mark 5:1-20	Jesus healed a man possessed.
DAY 11	John 2:1-11	Jesus turned water into wine.

DAY 12	Mark 6:30-44	*Jesus fed a crowd of five thousand with five loaves and two fish.*
DAY 13	John 9	*Jesus gave sight to a man born blind.*
DAY 14	John 21	*Jesus rose from the dead.*

Chapter 17: The Gospel of Matthew

DAY 1	Matt. 1:1-17; Luke 3:23-38	*Two accounts of his genealogy.*
DAY 2	Matt. 4:1-17; Mark 1:12-13; Luke 4:1-13	*Three accounts of his temptation.*
DAY 3	Matt. 26:57-56; Mark 14:43-52; Luke 22:47-53; John 18:1-11	*Four accounts of the betrayal and arrest of Jesus.*
DAY 4	Matt. 5:1-20	*The Beatitudes; salt and light; righteousness.*
DAY 5	Matt. 5:21-48	*Anger, adultery, and divorce; oaths, retaliation, enemies.*
DAY 6	Matt. 6:1-18	*Almsgiving, prayer, and fasting.*
DAY 7	Matt. 6:19-34	*Treasures, anxiety.*
DAY 8	Matt. 7:1-14	*Judging, profaning the holy, the narrow gate.*
DAY 9	Matt. 7:15-29	*"I never knew you"; house on a rock.*
DAY 10	Matt. 16:13-23	*Peter's confession.*
DAY 11	Matt. 23:1-36	*The scribes and Pharisees.*
DAY 12	Matt. 25:1-14	*Parable of the ten bridesmaids.*
DAY 13	Matt. 25:14-30	*Parable of the talents.*
DAY 14	Matt. 25:31-46	*Parable of "the least of these my brothers and sisters."*

Chapter 18: The Gospel of Mark

DAY 1	Mark 7:24-30	*Jesus cured the daughter of a Syrophoenician woman.*
DAY 2	Mark 8:27–9:1	*Peter's confession.*
DAY 3	Mark 11:1-11	*Jesus entered into Jerusalem.*
DAY 4	Mark 12:1-12	*Parable of the wicked tenants.*
DAY 5	Mark 12:13-15	*About paying taxes.*

DAY 6	Mark 12:18-27	*About the resurrection.*
DAY 7	Mark 12:28-34	*About the first commandment.*
DAY 8	Mark 13:1-27	*Jesus told of the persecution to come.*
DAY 9	Mark 13:28-37	*Jesus urged watchfulness.*
DAY 10	Mark 14:1-31	*Anointing, passover, Judas.*
DAY 11	Mark 14:32-52	*Jesus' prayer; his betrayal and arrest.*
DAY 12	Mark 14:53–15:5	*Examination and trial.*
DAY 13	Mark 15:6-47	*Jesus was crucified, dead, and buried.*
DAY 14	Mark 16:1-8	*Three women found his tomb empty.*

Chapter 19: The Gospel of Luke

DAY 1	Luke 4:16-30	*Jesus' sermon in the Nazareth synagogue.*
DAY 2	Luke 9:18-27	*Peter's declaration.*
DAY 3	Luke 10:25-37	*Jesus told the story of a Samaritan.*
DAY 4	Luke 13:22-30	*The last will be first, and the first last.*
DAY 5	Luke 15:1-10	*Two parables: lost sheep and lost coin.*
DAY 6	Luke 15:11-32	*The prodigal son.*
DAY 7	Luke 16:1-13	*Parable about wealth.*
DAY 8	Luke 16:19-31	*The rich man and Lazarus.*
DAY 9	Luke 17:11-19	*A tale about giving thanks.*
DAY 10	Luke 18:1-8	*A tale about persistence in prayer.*
DAY 11	Luke 22:1-23	*The Lord's supper.*
DAY 12	Luke 22:24-62	*Jesus and his disciples.*
DAY 13	Luke 23:1-25	*The trials.*
DAY 14	Luke 23:26-56	*Crucified, dead, and buried.*

Chapter 20: The Gospel of John

DAY 1	John 2	*The wedding at Cana.*
DAY 2	John 3:1-21	*Visit from Nicodemus.*
DAY 3	John 4:1-42	*The woman of Samaria.*
DAY 4	John 6:60-71	*The words of eternal life.*
DAY 5	John 8:12-20	*The light of the world.*
DAY 6	John 9	*Jesus healed a man born blind.*
DAY 7	John 10:1-21	*The good shepherd.*
DAY 8	John 11:1-44	*Jesus raised Lazarus from the dead.*

DAY 9	John 13:1-20	*Jesus washed the disciples' feet.*
DAY 10	John 14:1-14	*The way, the truth, and the life.*
DAY 11	John 14:15-31	*The promise of the Holy Spirit.*
DAY 12	John 15:1-17	*The true vine.*
DAY 13	John 17	*Jesus prayed for his disciples.*
DAY 14	John 18:12–19:42	*His trial, death, and burial.*

Chapter 21: The Resurrection

DAY 1	Matt. 27:62-66	*Pilate made sure.*
DAY 2	Matt. 28:1-10	*"He is not here."*
DAY 3	Matt. 28:11-15	*Keeping out of trouble.*
DAY 4	Matt. 28:16-20	*The great commission.*
DAY 5	Luke 24:1-12	*The report of three women.*
DAY 6	Luke 24:13-35	*On the road to Emmaus.*
DAY 7	Luke 24:36-49	*Jesus appeared to his disciples.*
DAY 8	Luke 24:50-53	*Jesus' ascension.*
DAY 9	John 20:1-10	*Empty tomb.*
DAY 10	John 20:11-18	*Jesus appeared to Mary Magdalene.*
DAY 11	John 20:19-29	*Jesus appeared to his disciples.*
DAY 12	John 20:30-31	*The purpose of this writing.*
DAY 13	John 21	*Jesus serves his disciples breakfast.*
DAY 14	1 Cor. 15:42-57	*"Death is swallowed up in victory!"*

Chapter 22: The Early Church

DAY 1	Acts 1	*Ascension of Jesus; replacing Judas.*
DAY 2	Acts 2	*Pentecost; Peter's courage; the first converts.*
DAY 3	Acts 3	*Speech in Solomon's portico.*
DAY 4	Acts 4:1-22	*Peter and John before the Jerusalem Council.*
DAY 5	Acts 4:23-37	*The new church shared their belongings.*
DAY 6	Acts 5:1-11	*The sad saga of Ananias and Sapphira.*
DAY 7	Acts 5:12-42	*Healings and persecution.*
DAY 8	Acts 6:1-7	*Servant leaders for the church.*
DAY 9	Acts 6:8–8:1a	*Stephen's faith and stoning.*
DAY 10	Acts 8:4-25	*Philip preached in Samaria.*
DAY 11	Acts 8:26-40	*Philip and the Ethiopian eunuch.*

DAY 12	Acts 10	Peter and the Roman centurion.
DAY 13	Acts 11:1-18	Peter's report to the church in Jerusalem.
DAY 14	Acts 12	Violence and growth.

Chapter 23: The Apostle Paul

DAY 1	Acts 8:1b-3; 9:1-31	Saul the devout Pharisee became Paul the devout apostle of Jesus Christ.
DAY 2	Acts 13	Saul and Barnabas, traveling missionaries.
DAY 3	Rom. 8:1-30	Life in the Spirit, and the Christian hope.
DAY 4	Rom. 8:31-39	The steadfast love of God in Jesus Christ.
DAY 5	Rom. 11	The wide perimeter of God's amazing love.
DAY 6	Rom. 12	"Do not be conformed to this world but be transformed."
DAY 7	1 Cor. 11:17-34	On eating and drinking at the table.
DAY 8	1 Cor. 12	The body and its many members.
DAY 9	1 Cor. 13	God's love.
DAY 10	1 Cor. 14	Gifts of prophecy and tongues in worship.
DAY 11	1 Cor. 15	Resurrection to life.
DAY 12	Eph. 6:10-20	"Put on the whole armor of God."
DAY 13	Phil. 2:1-18	Christ poured himself out.
DAY 14	Phil. 3:1–4:7	Pressing on.

Chapter 24: The Destruction of Jerusalem and the Revelation

DAY 1	Rev. 1	Introduction; a vision of the Son of Man.
DAY 2	Rev. 4	Worship in heaven.
DAY 3	Rev. 5	The lamb's scroll.
DAY 4	Rev. 6	The seven seals.
DAY 5	Rev. 7	The elect, from Israel and from the nations.
DAY 6	Rev. 8–9	Seven trumpets.
DAY 7	Rev. 13	The beasts.
DAY 8	Rev. 14	The lamb with 144,000; three angels.
DAY 9	Rev. 15	Seven plagues.
DAY 10	Rev. 16	Bowls of God's wrath.
DAY 11	Rev. 17	The whore and the beast.
DAY 12	Rev. 18	The fall of Babylon and all it represents.

| DAY 13 | Rev. 19 | *Rejoicing and victory.* |
| DAY 14 | Rev. 21:9–22:5 | *The vision of the second creation.* |

Chapter 25: The Whole Story's Meaning: Psalm 90

DAY 1	Psalm 90	*God's eternity and our brevity.*
DAY 2	Psalm 103	*God's goodness to us.*
DAY 3	Psalm 61	*"Let me abide in your tent forever."*
DAY 4	Psalm 62	*"For God alone my soul waits."*
DAY 5	Psalm 63	*"My soul thirsts for you."*
DAY 6	Psalm 88	*"Why do you cast me off?"*
DAY 7	Psalm 91	*God's protection.*
DAY 8	Psalm 93	*The majesty of God.*
DAY 9	Psalm 97	*The Lord reigns!*
DAY 10	Psalm 104	*The greatness of God.*
DAY 11	Psalm 111	*"Great are the works of the Lord."*
DAY 12	Psalm 121	*"The Lord is your keeper."*
DAY 13	Psalm 145	*"All your works shall give thanks to you."*
DAY 14	Eccles. 2	*A description of the futility we sometimes feel.*

Chapter 26: One Story: God's Call

DAY 1	1 Samuel 3	*God called Samuel.*
DAY 2	Amos 7:10-17	*God called Amos.*
DAY 3	Jer. 1:4-19	*God called Jeremiah.*
DAY 4	Ezek. 1	*God called Ezekiel.*
DAY 5	Zech. 1:1-6	*God called Zechariah, the prophet.*
DAY 6	Mark 2:13-17	*God called Levi, the tax collector.*
DAY 7	Luke 1:5-20	*God called Zechariah, the father of John the Baptist.*
DAY 8	Luke 1:26-38	*God called Mary.*
DAY 9	Luke 5:1-11	*God called Jesus' disciples.*
DAY 10	John 1:35-42	*God called the first disciples of Jesus.*
DAY 11	John 1:43-51	*God called Philip and Nathaniel.*
DAY 12	Acts 16:11-15	*God called Lydia.*
DAY 13	Rev. 1:9-20	*God called John of the Revelation.*
DAY 14	Heb. 11:1–12:2	*The "great cloud of witnesses" that answered God's call.*

Index